LOST IN THE STORM

LOST IN THE STORM

STORM

FROM PRISON TO THE PULPIT

DAVID ROCHA

PARAKLETOS PUBLISHING
MODESTO

CONTENTS

INTRODUCTION

Hello and thank you for picking up my book. I never thought I would actually finish this project that began in solitary confinement. I don't know if I began writing this book for publishing, or if I just began writing my story so I wouldn't go insane in my cell. I was given an eight-year federal prison sentence and served six of those years. Many times I've shared my story with friends or congregations, and am told that it sounds like a movie. I don't quite understand how I lived through most of it. All I can say is that God kept me safe and alive through it all for such a time as this. This story needs to be told in order to reach many for Jesus. That is my sole purpose in writing this book, to reach you.

It has been ten years since I no longer belonged to the Federal Bureau of Prisons. At the time I hated every second I spent in prison, only now can I see the wisdom of God allowing me to be there for a time. He was building me up with a purpose. I have met so many good brothers while incarcerated. Most of them are free now and still serving the Lord with all of their hearts. I believe that God is building an army within the prison walls that will not be compromised by the world. We are survivors.

This is not a book that details or implicates anyone. It is simply a book that points to a good, amazing, patient loving God named Jesus Christ.

David Rocha
www.houseofrestchurch.com

FOREWORD

When you know why you exist, everything begins to make sense and fall into place. Until then, you just have to figure things out for yourself. It is one thing to look back over the years with a mature perspective and see things with clarity, it's quite another to be a young man looking toward the future and having no idea what to expect. The Bible says that God knows the end from the beginning, which makes perfect sense to me now. I reflect on how God has worked things out in the lives of so many people I know.

You'll see what I am talking about as you read this book. What you hold in your hands is not a made-up story, on the contrary, it is very real. I've been friends with Pastor David and his wife Sharon for a few years now. I have had the privilege of being able to sit and talk with them in their home. The stories you are going to come across in this book are going to stir something in you. you are going to see that just as God has a plan for your life, so does the devil. The beautiful thing about it all is that God is relentless in his love for you. He will continue to pursue you for all the days of your life.

This book provides a clear picture of how God works and what it looks like for God to pursue a man. In this story, you are going to hear the first-hand account of a man that has tasted the fame, power, and respect that the world has to offer. You are also going to hear how those things do not satisfy.

One thing I've always heard that has stuck to my mind is this. *'The devil wants to build you up just to tear you down, but God will tear you down just to build you up.'* What this means to me is that the devil lures us into lifestyles that we think we want. Only to find out that what you get isn't really what you truly wanted. The devil may win a few battles, but ultimately, it's Jesus that wins the war.

As you walk through this story, I want you to think about your life, the ups and downs, and about what you've learned along your own personal journey. As you contemplate this, I want you to know that in the same way God was with David throughout his life, God is with you also.

By the time you finish reading this, I pray that you are able to see God's ways more clearly in your own life. If you are already a believer in Christ, you know what I am talking about. If you've never considered surrendering your heart to Jesus, I pray that you do. It will be the best decision you've ever made in your life.

Carlos Garcia

1

THE CRAZY PLACE

Lock it down now!" echoed loudly through the pod. I tried my hardest to ignore the yelling. "I said to lock it down!" demanded the officer.

Unable to continue reading, I put down my Bible and sat up from my bunk. I slowly walked over to my cell door to look out my thin window and into the pod. An argument was quickly escalating as Rico refused to lock down after his hour of pod time. *I know what comes next*, I dreaded.

"My hour isn't up! I was on the phone with my grandmother! And you can't even warn me! You just shut the phones off!" screamed Rico at the top of his lungs.

Rico pulled his shirt off, ready to do battle. The officer stood on the opposite side of the thick glass, looking into the half-circle pod with eighteen cells. Within minutes I knew officers would come rushing in with riot gear: billy clubs and flash-bang grenades. Rico began pacing the pod like an angry lion, psyching himself up for the inevitable. *What does it matter anyway since he's facing twenty to life for murder?* I thought. I whispered a prayer for him.

Life in solitary confinement is inhumane. The hatred it breeds boils like lava ready to explode at the smallest disrespect. Nerves are always on edge and fuses are short. I was about to witness another eruption.

"Here they come! Here they come!" yelled someone from a cell in the top tier. Ten officers dressed in black riot gear complete with shields and masks stood ready at the door to rush in. By this time Rico had run into his cell, came out with bottles of shampoo from the commissary, and began pouring it on the floor next to each door, making it slippery for the officers as they rushed in. The first officer was holding a rifle with flashbangs.

"Come on! I'll take one of you down!" yelled Rico as he balled his fists, ready to swing.

The door popped open and the officer shot the flashbang toward Rico. Instantly the pod was filled with smoke, giving it the effect of a war zone. The officers rushed in screaming "Lay down!" Every inmate began pounding their doors and yelling, which made the entire moment seem like a madhouse. Rico swung and connected with the head of the first officer, sending his face shield flying across the pod. The second officer swung and hit Rico with his baton. Adrenaline and rage were so high that the blow didn't even faze him. Rico's muscles ripped with veins pulsing as if hot venom was traveling throughout his body. Rico somehow grabbed an officer in a chokehold and tried his hardest to squeeze the life out of him. With gritted teeth, he hollered, "All I wanted was to say goodbye! See what you made me do!"

"Let him go! Let him go now!" one officer screamed. The pounding from the inmates became louder. Officers began hitting his legs, back, and arms with their batons. The blows only enraged him more, causing his squeeze on the officer's neck to get tighter. The officer began to turn purple and his eyes began rolling into his head. With no other alternative, an officer pulled back his baton and hit Rico square on the back of his head. The sound of the baton to skull seemed to override all other sounds. Rico's hold released as he fell forward, unconscious. The officers swung and struck a few more blows at his limp body, then cuffed him and carried him off.

As quickly as it began, it ended. The only evidence was a smoke-filled pod. The inmates stopped yelling and kicking their doors, and all was eerily silent. With more frustration than shock, I sat back down on my bunk. "When will this nightmare end?" I asked myself. I was thankful there was an end for me. Some men I've met will never walk into freedom. I at least had a release date. It's unbelievable how many times in the past this could have been a permanent home for me, but God had other plans even though I didn't know it. Let me rephrase that: I knew God had plans for me; I just chose to ignore Him.

We find God in places we'd least expect. Moses found God in the backside of the desert, watching his father-in-law's sheep. Peter found God while pulling up to shore with empty nets after a long night of hard work. A criminal found God while he was being crucified next to Him on a hill named Golgotha. Isaiah 55:8 says, "for my thoughts are not your thoughts, neither are your ways my ways." The same rings true today. We find God on battlefields thousands of miles from home, on deathbeds, in car accidents, through lost jobs, or after the death of a loved one. God seems to show up during our darkest and most hopeless times, as a light showing us the path. In actuality, God has always been there; we just weren't looking.

That brings us to my story. I didn't find God in a church or a parking lot revival. I found Him in solitary confinement, a place more commonly known as "the hole." The phrase "found God" isn't actually correct, however, because to find God implies that God was lost; it's us sinners who are the lost sheep. So the correct term should be "He found me." After years of running and hiding from Him, I slammed right into Him in prison.

It was evening time in this hell on earth, tucked inside the massive compound. The jail was surrounded by fences and razor-sharp barbed wire. I was beyond several steel doors and the general population pods, deep inside the building through the long, silent corridors. The "hole" was filled with murderers, rapists, mafia gang leaders, cop killers, drug cartel members and your average violent anti-social maniac who can't be housed in general-population pods because they were too vicious, too manipulative, or too powerful.

I and others alongside me were housed in single cells, which means we had no cellmates. We were kept from one another like Siamese Fighting Fish. We each got one hour outside our cells twice a week, but still within the locked pod. It was the only time we could shower, shave, and use the payphone. We each took turns coming out on an hourly rotation. Two inmates were never out together because allowing contact could have been fatal. Rapists, child molesters, rival gangs and rival drug dealers, as well as racists, were automatically targeted.

We were fed three times a day through slots in the centers of our cell doors. My cell was built with a toilet and sink combination, a concrete table, a metal stool welded to the floor, and a concrete bed with a mattress thinner than my Bible. I had a limited view of the outside through a narrow piece of five-inch glass. I seldom looked outside since my view was composed of a large fence, barbed wire, and sky.

Through a control booth, officers monitored six different pods built into a circle around them. This monitoring system wasn't always successful, however, with so many pods and inmates to watch. Men found ways to hang themselves and not be discovered for hours. One of my friends did it before I was put in "the hole." I still pray for his family and try not to think of the times we laughed and talked of the day we'd be free. That was before he was sentenced to life. That night he called his family and said goodbye, walked to his cell and hanged himself. He was found dead the next morning.

I am in no way encouraging suicide, but I can see

how dark and twisted a mind can become in a place like "the hole," where hope means nothing and the sane can quickly go insane. It is the belly of the beast, the gates of hell itself. Without God, we have no chance against Satan. This is Satan's playground: his games, his rules, and he plays for keeps.

Spending days, weeks, and months sitting in a cell alone does something to the human mind. I've seen strong-willed men mentally break. They begin talking to themselves, barking like dogs or screaming for hours as they sit in a dark cold cell week after week. I've learned how to spot a man on the verge of losing reality. He first begins to talk differently and walk differently; I can almost sense him withdrawing into himself. Others fight from going insane with anger and hatred. They'll lose all remorse and compassion because it's easier not to care. So they learn to have no mercy.

Officers approached us with caution and fear. We were shackled to our visits, shackled to the nurse, and shackled to court. We were treated like animals, so most of us began to act like animals. I was in constant spiritual battle daily.

Even in Christ I felt suffocated by the evil presence in the "hole." I constantly prayed for strength. I longed to fellowship with another Christian for support. I longed to hold my children, who I haven't touched in two years; I fought to stay afloat in the lake of despair. Sometimes I would realize days had passed since I'd last spoken to anyone. Sleeping became a challenge between the yelling, cursing, arguing, screaming, door banging, and meals. Sometimes even getting a full night's sleep became impossible.

At the beginning of my incarceration, I cherished my sleep; it was the only way to escape my surroundings and situation. I'd dream of my family and the fun times we'd had. Later my dreams turned into nightmares of corpses, death, disasters, violence, pain, and terror. I woke up shaking in fear because I had nightmares of demons chasing me through a forest with no end. *What is happening to me?* I thought. So, I started praying for Jesus to watch over me while I slept. I didn't know what was worse, being awake in the living horror of "the hole" or living through the horrors in my mind while I slept. It's impossible to fully describe how it feels to be isolated from the world.

Allow me to introduce myself, my name is David Rocha, but most know me as 'Dyno'. I was born in 1972, a Chicano from California's agricultural central valley. Born and raised in the small town of Tracy. I've been locked down for two years now, with eight of those months in the 'hole'. I stopped

13

running from Christ in a jail cell, I couldn't run anymore.

I led a life of fame, violence, crime, money, and drugs. Yes, I was an addict, but not in the same sense that most are addicted. You see, I wasn't addicted to drugs physically; I was addicted to the power and money that came from selling them. The rush of standing on stage at a concert, the rush of meeting my drug connection in secret places, the rush of weighing meth on a triple beam scale, or the rush of having the power to hurt an enemy at my whim. It was the addiction, my rush. I loved it and couldn't stop even if I wanted to. Yes, I was just as addicted as the tweakers I sold to, but money was my fix and I could never have enough of it. I can lie and say violence was avoided when possible. To be honest, I loved the violence; to beat, hurt, intimidate and threaten was power. In a perfect drug dealing world, all ran smoothly, but that was not always the case. Someone was always out to take your place, to give better prices or to get better quality. It was just part of life, and I was good at it.

I was a part of the last generation of the old school cholo, dressed in perfectly ironed and creased Ben Davis pants and white T-shirts, Chicano slang and lowriders with hydraulics. A time of cruising strips filled with 'Raza' A place you could meet a 'firme jaina' and be in a shoot-out on the same street. A place of homegirls with heavy make-up and teased hair. All of the so-called innocent times had long passed, my generation brought in the dark times. Times of drive-by's, murders with no mercy, manipulation, conspiracy; times of using drugs to control entire cities. We believed in power by force, power only money could buy. It was all downhill from then on, each generation was twice as ruthless.

I'm sorry; I'm getting ahead of myself, aren't I? My story doesn't begin in a drug-infested California town. It begins with a young boy of eight in a small Christian church. So relax, be patient and travel back with me to 1980 in downtown Stockton California. May God show you his message through my testimony. Ultimately this story isn't about me; it's about a true living God that loved us enough to die for us two thousand years ago, a God that rose again after three days and lives forever, making a way for us to receive salvation. This story is of hardship, sorrow and sin, conquered by hope, forgiveness, and love. Jesus Christ, the same yesterday, today and forever.

1980

It was a small brick building in the middle of a drug-infested downtown area. It might have been an office in the past but now it was a small Holy Spirit filled church. It wasn't much but to the congregation, it was a place of peace, fellowship, salvation, worship, and hope. Instead of the traditional long wooden church pews, it contained mismatched metal fold up chairs. There was a small stage for an altar and an old used PA system for guitars and microphones. The songs and sermons were in Spanish and the basement was used for children's bible study. It wasn't big, lavish or fancy but it was comfortable. People tend to believe that the bigger and fancier a church is that the more God's presence is there. God doesn't measure dedication by material worldly things. The presence of the Lord is unlimited, from the White House to the crack house. The Lord goes where the door is opened to Him. The church would fill with 60 people, most middle class or poor and everyone wore their Sunday best, including my family. In attendance were my father, mother and my little brother Angel and myself. My two older brothers hardly attended with us, they were teenagers too busy for church.

My mother accepted Christ when I was five years old. In the beginning, only my mother and I attended church. I didn't like it or dislike it. The sermons were usually boring but the songs were fun to clap to plus I loved being with my mother. She taught me all the stories of the Bible. Adam and Eve to the Apostle Paul, I loved hearing them. I knew God was real even at the young age of eight years old. My mother was baptized in water while pregnant with my younger brother Angel. Even though I believed the stories in the Bible it wasn't until I witnessed a true miracle with my own eyes that I truly believed.

My father was an alcoholic yet always maintained his job and provided. My memories of my father were with a beer can in his hand. He always drank after work, at home, driving, every weekend every day. Even though he continued drinking and smoking my mother continued praying for him with me. I shared a bedroom with my oldest brother Ruben, we had bunk beds and I had the lower bed. At night my father would stumble drunk into our bedroom and he'd cry to my oldest brother and I'd pretend to be asleep.

"Son, don't be like me, don't ever drink," my father would groan. "I want to change... I want to stop... I want to be a father my sons can respect, instead, I'm a drunk...please promise me you won't start drinking."

My brother wouldn't respond, he was seventeen years old. I would usually just fall asleep and not

17

even notice when he would leave to stumble back down the hall into his own bedroom to sleep. No matter how much he cried I knew he would be drinking the next day anyway. I would silently pray to Jesus for my dad to stop. I didn't even understand if and why drinking was bad, but I did know that it made my mom cry. Yet the days and weeks would be the same, and nothing would change.

Now as we sat in church once again, my dad attended. He began attending a little more regularly, yet his drinking had not stopped. This Sunday didn't feel any different from any other Sunday service. Little did I know that I was about to witness my first miracle.

"Who is tired of the heavy loads of this life? Who wants to be free! Jesus Christ died for your sins on a hill named Golgotha, and after three days He was raised again. Jesus is alive! He wants to bless you with a good life. He can free you from the bondage of Satan. He can break the chains of drugs, alcohol, pride, and hate. Accept Jesus Christ today because tomorrow isn't promised... come to the altar if you want to have a relationship with Jesus. Take the first step!" said the visiting evangelist at the end of his sermon. He continued,

"If you want prayer, come to the front right now. Do you want a miracle?"

Men, women, and children walked to the altar. My father didn't budge. All he was thinking about was buying a beer after service. He knew that when it was altar call time, that service was about to be over. He was feeling thirsty and was already imagining that cold beer hitting his lips. The pastor was praying for the people that had walked up to the front of the church, then the strangest thing happened. As he was praying for people he stopped and looked up to stare directly at my dad. After a moment he motioned for my dad to come forward. Time went into slow motion. In the first few seconds, my dad thought the pastor was signaling someone else, maybe someone behind him or around him. My dad was the only person in that direction. To his own surprise, he walked up to the evangelist.

"Are you saved?" asked the man.

My dad did not want to lie to God or himself anymore. Flashes of his life went through his mind like the stills of an old 16mm film. Thoughts of his family, his future, of the beer he drinks out of the addiction more than the pleasure. So many times he would stumble in our bedroom, ashamed of his drunkenness with his empty promises to stop drinking.

He looked at the evangelist and said, "No."

Then the pastor asked my dad one more straight

to the point question. "Would you like to accept Jesus Christ today as your personal savior?"

My dad, sick and tired of running from God answered, "Yes."

And in a small Stockton California church, my dad was born again. In the snap of a finger, his desires for liquor, smoking and worldly music died. He was set free and to this day has never touched liquor again. It was my first miracle I had ever witnessed what the power of God can do.

Things got much better at home when both of my parents were following Jesus Christ, and I thank God for the examples they were to me as I grew up. Yet this wasn't the happily ever after ending that movies tend to have. There was a heavy influence that still seemed to creep into our home during the early 80s. All children are influenced by what surrounds them while growing up. In the 80s, any Chicano neighborhood in California was filled with cholos, cholas, and lowriders. The cholo had a certain air and pride about him. A certain walk and talk. Head always held high with Chicano pride. I was fascinated by the mystery the cholos projected. I couldn't wait to grow up to be a cholo. Of course, all of this was through the eyes of a young impressionable boy. Too innocent to know the dark side of the vida loca. The gang fights, the stabbings, the paint sniffing, and weed smoking. Also the jails and prisons full of cholos joining prison gangs. Most of the young cholos in the late 70s and early 80s went to prison with release dates in the late 80s and 90s. What I didn't realize was releasing with these men, were all of the prison politics and rules. A new wave of violence was about to erupt out of the prisons and into our neighborhood streets.

Little did my generation know the trap that Satan had set up for us. Within a few years, gang violence would reach an all-time high. During this time, I had no idea of the fight for my soul that laid before me. I realize now in looking back that through my parents, God was preparing me spiritually. This world has always been a spiritual battleground, between good and evil. Most wars are fought for territory, but the enemy's spiritual war is a fight for our souls. We have a fight against an enemy that does not fight fairly. He does not abide by any rules of engagement, or with any type of mercy. There are no innocent bystanders and no place sacred. Satan hates us and will use anything to distract us from Jesus. It can be drugs, gangs, hate, greed, witchcraft, fornication, riches or even religion. He sets out to destroy the very fabric of our home and family. He poisons the minds of children before they even have a chance, and by doing that, he is destroying future believers, future pastors, and future men and women of God. The cycle never ends until the family breaks down into crumbs and dust. All that is left are lost sheep wandering in the wilderness. Without Jesus, we have no protection from the roaring lion.

Ephesians 6:12 says, *"For we wrestle not against flesh and blood, but against the principalities, against powers, against the rulers of the darkness of this world, against spiritual wickedness in high places."*

2

ENEMY OF THE STATE

I wake up once again in my small cell in solitary confinement. I have my daily program. In my opinion, each inmate needs to program. Not for anyone else, but for your own sanity. Let me explain for those that have never served time, much less in isolation. Without a program, you lose complete sense of time. The minutes, hours, days and months slip by. It all becomes one big eternity with no beginning and no end. One might think this wouldn't be a problem, but it is exactly what can drive a man to lose his mind. It is like having no map or GPS and no type of landmark to at least recognize where you are or what direction you are going. To this day I truly believe that solitary confinement is a type of torture that leaves no bruises or scars that are visible by the human eye. Yet this is what is done to thousands of inmates that will one day be released back into society and into our streets and cities. The best thing an inmate can do is to have a daily program.

I will describe my own personal program to give you a better idea of what I am talking about. In the morning I'm awakened by the officers serving breakfast. I hear the wheels of the food cart being brought into my unit. Then I hear the giant keys opening the slots of each cell one at a time. The sound gets louder as the officer gets closer to my own cell. The slot in my door swings inward and becomes a sort of shelf or small table just wide enough to hold the food tray. Due to the fact that I am in solitary confinement, it takes quite a bit of time to serve each inmate. It reminds me of my childhood when my dad raised pigs and would serve them food in their trough every day at the same time. It was like clockwork as the pigs would get excited when my dad would walk up to their pig pen to feed them. I get up from my bunk, which was nothing less than a concrete bed with a mattress about three inches thick. Of course, the mattress was about one inch thick once I laid on it. I grab the tray of food and put it on my table that was attached to the wall by giant bolts. I quickly wash up and sit on my stool that was also connected to the floor with giant bolts. I pray and thank God for the food and eat my breakfast. There is always an orange or an apple, I always save that for a snack later on in the day. Once breakfast was over I clean up my cell which included cleaning my floor, my sink and toilet and making up my bed. Then I open my bible and study and read until lunch time. Once lunch came, which consisted of a bagged lunch of two sandwiches, a small carton of fruit punch and another piece of fruit. When lunch was served you had to make sure to be at your door. Since it wasn't served in a tray, the officer would open the slot and just throw the lunch bag on the floor and quickly close the slot so they could get to the next cell. There is something so degrading when that happens. For me, the worst part of lunch is the two sandwiches, with only one small packet of mayonnaise. Either I would spread the single packet over both sandwiches and hardly taste anything besides the dry bread, or I spread it over one sandwich and actually taste the mayo in one of them and the other sandwich I would just eat it dry. Today I actually got one packet of Mayonnaise and one packet of mustard. Feels like a five-star lunch if you ask me.

Once lunch is over I take a short nap. Now half of my day is over with and I'm glad. Every twenty-four hours that pass was one day closer to being released and free. One day closer to holding my children, one day closer to serving God in an actual church building and having someone to fellowship with. After my nap, I wake up and write letters to my children, to my parents or brothers. I made it a priority to write my children almost daily for the entire time I would be incarcerated. I didn't want them to forget me. My youngest daughter was too young to read so I draw her pictures of cartoons and color them in for her along with a small note on the corner of how much I love her. By the time I was finished with my letters and they were sealed and addressed I spend some more time in the bible before dinner. Once dinner comes it was basically the same routine as breakfast, with the slot of the door brought down and the food tray served. When dinner was over it was time for me to either draw or read a novel for my enjoyment and entertainment. A book cart was always in the unit and was usually changed out every week or so with different books that were on rotation from other units. It was actually exciting when we get a book cart, it's one of my highlights during my time in this hell hole. Sometimes there are even classics by one of my favorite authors, like John Steinbeck. My day always ended with prayer. I would pray for each of my

children and family members and others that were
on my heart. It was also during the late nights that
I write sermons so I could send them to my mom
and dad. What I just described to you is my program.
My program might not be the same as my neighbors
around me, but one way or another you had to have
a program. It was either that or within weeks you'd
find yourself yelling and kicking your door for no
reason for hours at a time. Sometimes screaming at
the top of your lungs. I've seen it happen more often
than I'd like to remember. My program is how I
break up my day, and most important of all is it keeps
my mind occupied. Of course, some days are harder
than others. Other small things helped break up the
days also. Such as every two or three days I'm given
an hour outside of my cell and I can use that time
to take a shower, use the phone or just walk around
in my unit. Also, each Thursday we get our
commissary. I always make sure to get a bag of
barbecue chips, my favorite. Plus three times a week
I get thirty-minute visits from my parents, family,
children or friends.

Since I have nothing but time, I want to
explain how I ended up in a place like this in the first
place. In 2001, I was on probation for a possession of
meth charge I caught back in 1999. I was out living
my life as a rapper, drug dealer and gangster. What I

didn't know was my entire world was about to come crashing down. Each month I was ordered to check in with my probation officer. By this time It had been over two years since I was on probation so I didn't even have to check-in personally anymore. I would simply mail in a form once a month. Answering questions like my address or an address change, and if I've had any contact with police. Life was busy with running the recording studio, writing new songs, producing tracks, promotion and marketing, meetings and either filming a new movie or preparing to film a new movie. Between all of these things, I had a great meth connection and a solid crew of homies moving the product. I didn't think much of it when I received a phone call from someone introducing themselves as my new probation officer. He said that he is new and is calling everyone on his caseload to come into the probation department so he can meet each person. He was being very cool and even allowed me to make an appointment for a time that I could come in to meet him. I told him I could make my way to the office the next morning.

The next day I got ready, picked up one of my best friends and we drove to Stockton. I figured I could quickly go to check in and maybe grab a bite to eat after. Nothing seemed out of the ordinary as

I waited for my name to be called. Once I walked into the door past the lobby and walked down the hallway into the building I was surrounded by the F.B.I. and a few detectives. I was quickly handcuffed and told that I have been indicted by the Federal Government. I was being arrested and charged under the RICO act (*The Racketeer Influenced and Corrupt Organizations Act*). 'This was crazy!' I thought to myself. I was taken to Sacramento County Jail and within a few hours, I found myself in the holding cell of the federal building next door to the jail with others that I was apparently indicted with. Guys I had never met or known. The Feds called it Operation Black Widow. Within a few days, I was transported to a jail in downtown Oakland and put in Solitary along with the other defendants in the case. I spent thirty days in the Oakland jail before I was released on a federal bond and put on Federal probation. I knew I wasn't perfect or an angel, but I knew that I had nothing to do with the things I was being charged with. I was going to fight this case to the end. And for the next three years, I fought this case with too many court dates to count. Each time I would have to go to the San Francisco Federal Court building along with my co-defendants as the prosecutor accused the group of things such as dealing drugs, robberies and even murder. It was a very crazy time for me as the lifestyle I was living was getting old. I began to feel trapped in the rap and drug world. I thought I was building an empire, but in reality, it was a prison that I was building all around me. I had no peace. My music was selling nationally and internationally along with our movies in every video store across the country. I felt as if the Feds were watching my every move and so were my enemies. I stopped trusting even my closest friends and I always had a feeling as if my life would end soon.

It was during this time that I made the dumbest mistake I had ever made. All because of a friend. I mean no harm to this person, because in the big picture if it wasn't for him I would have never been in a place to call out to God. I would have never humbled my heart to Jesus and as far as I know, maybe I wouldn't be alive today. I thought I was doing a friend a favor by helping him get some crystal meth to sell so he could feed his kids. Everything in me told me not to do it. I was on federal probation and my entire life was on the line. Actually, because of my federal indictment and being released on a federal bond, I no longer had a meth connection. I went against my better judgment and after many requests from him I figured out how to get him what he wanted. The entire time I was being filmed and audio recorded by the F.B.I.

I still remember that day clearly. After the deal, I didn't feel right. My hands were shaking and I couldn't figure out why. I knew that something was wrong. I was so tired of this life. So tired of claiming a gang, so tired of being this rap artist. I just wanted to be David. I wanted to raise my kids and be normal. Even get a regular 9 to 5 job. I went home and sat on the couch, feeling uneasy. I felt restless and didn't know why I was feeling this way. After a few minutes, I called my parents.

"Mom," I said into my phone

"Yes mijo, is everything ok? It's late," she said.

I had totally forgotten about the time and realized that I must have startled her. I continued to talk to her without wanting to explain what I just did.

"Mom... can you both come over to pray for me and the house. I don't feel right and I feel like something evil is here," I said.

"Okay, we'll be right over," answered my mom. I felt a little better. I had bought a house about three miles away from my parents, so I knew it wouldn't take them long to arrive. I paced my house back and forth feeling like something bad was happening. The mother of my children was feeling nervous because she had never seen me lose my cool like this. Finally, after roughly fifteen minutes I heard their car pull into my driveway. I walked over to open the front door for them and realized they had also brought along my younger brother Angel who was a youth pastor at this point with a church in Stockton. I didn't realize they would be bringing him and I felt glad he came also. I didn't know how to explain what I was feeling but I told them I needed prayer and the house needed to be prayed for.

"Something evil is in this house, especially by my studio. I can feel it... can't you feel it!" I asked as I pointed to the room where my music studio was at. Angel didn't acknowledge whether he did or not but I followed him as we went from room to room so he could pray. Angel and my parents first went to the bedrooms and prayed, then prayed over the children and the living room and dining room. Finally was my recording studio was last. I didn't understand why but I felt afraid as we stepped into there. The moment Angel began praying in the studio my knees buckled and I fell down weeping. I wanted this evil presence gone from my house and from my children. A spiritual war was happening in my home with my brother Angel and my parents. The more they prayed the better I began to feel. I could literally feel the darkness begin to rise and leave my home. Once Angel stopped praying, he said,

"David, this isn't about your house. This is about you. Jesus wants you. Are you ready to accept Him into your heart."

I was heartbroken because I knew I wasn't ready to change. I said, "I can't."

"David, this is the only way. Jesus is the only way. Only He can change your heart."

I shook my head over and over. "I can't... I can't." Then I said, "But I am done doing the things I was doing. I quit it all. I quit the gangs, I'll quit making music or rapping. I am done. I will find a job to provide for my family and I will go to church each Sunday."

I'm sure as I said this, it broke my parent's hearts and my brother's. There was a breakthrough in my home that day, but my heart was still hard. My pride was too big. They stayed for a bit longer and they left home. My hands had stopped shaking and I went to sleep with peace in my heart. I really meant it when I said I was going to stop everything and change.

As the weeks passed I attended church on Sundays. Usually, I'd go alone unless I had my older daughters with me. I would take them with me and enjoy the day with them. I began looking for work by filling out applications and had actually got hired by a home loan broker. Things were looking promising. Yet after about a month of attending church with my parents, I began finding excuses for showing up late to service, or not showing up at all. Even though I stopped living a bad lifestyle, I realized that it was still in my heart. Just because I wasn't doing it, didn't mean the desire had left. Now in looking back, I realize that I was trying to change myself. I was trying to change my behavior. Changing one's behavior is not Christianity. Christianity is not putting a leash on your impulses and just being the best you. Is a drug addict still a drug addict if he desires it yet has none? Just because he stays away from it does not mean he is delivered from it. Jesus can do nothing without a surrendered heart. This was a hard lesson I still had yet to learn. All of these things happened in December of 2003. By February 2004 I had completely stopped attending church service with my parents until a week after my youngest daughter turned one year old.

It was a typical Sunday and of course, I was late. I knew that the songs at the beginning of the service usually lasted about thirty minutes. I planned on showing up late so I wouldn't have to stand and clap the entire time. When I showed up to the church building, the parking lot was completely full and I contemplated leaving. I decided to stay and park in the overflow parking lot furthest from the church. When I entered inside, the church was full to the brim. If I recall right, the building seated over 500 people and I was ushered to the very back of the sanctuary where they had put out some overflow chairs. To be honest, I hardly paid any attention to the sermon. I knew that God was real but I just couldn't take the step. I felt as if I was stone when it came to the things of God. I would see people smile, cry or worship the Lord and I couldn't understand why I felt nothing. Before I realized, the sermon was over and the pastor gave the microphone over to my brother Angel. He didn't know I was in the building and neither did my parents who were sitting a few rows from the front of the church.

"How would you worship God if you knew he would answer your prayer!" yelled Angel on the microphone. People began to shout as the musicians began to slowly play music. Then out of nowhere, he called my father up to the front of the church.

"Dad, how would you dance for the Lord if it meant the salvation of your sons?"

Then what I saw will forever be etched into my heart. The moment Angel said that, my dad began jumping and kicking his legs and waving his arms like a crazy man. He wouldn't stop dancing and spinning. To the non-believer, he looked insane. But to me, sitting in the back of the church watching my dad dancing, for the salvation of his sons. It broke me. It shattered me. It humbled me. My dad's dance did something no sermon, no bible study, no talks had ever done in all the years of my life. It felt like a giant chisel was aimed at my heart and the very hand of God struck that chisel all the way to the core of my being. I wanted to scream and run to the front to dance with him. I wanted to shout and cry out to Jesus. I wanted my dad to know that I loved him too... But I didn't budge, I didn't move and I didn't even allow one single tear to fall from my eye. From the outside, I looked like a stone cold gangster. Inside I was shattered into pieces by the love of a father for his son. I had no idea that I was about to be served with a federal indictment within a few days and I would lose my freedom for years to come.

3

NOT EVEN GOD
CAN HELP HIM

FEB 25TH 2004

It was a typical weekday morning for me, besides the fact that my son had just started kindergarten. Usually, I would stay up all night in the studio and still be awake when it was time to take him. Once I would take him to school I would come home and fall asleep for a few hours before I started my day all over again. I was tired and a bit sleepy while I drove my son which was roughly five minutes away. I told him I loved him as I dropped him off. I made sure to stay there until I saw him open the door of his classroom and walk in. As I drove back toward my house I didn't notice anything different. As soon as I turned on my street I saw patrol lights behind me. I pulled over to the side of the road. I didn't notice the undercover cars until the officer actually pulled me out of my car. All of a sudden I was completely surrounded by about a dozen officers. Some in uniform but most of them in plain clothes. A few had F.B.I. or D.E.A. on their jackets as they began to search through my car. I was completely confused, which is exactly what they wanted. A detective put me into an unmarked car and one of the other detectives took my keys and we all made a caravan to my house.

I found myself handcuffed and sitting on one of my couches as officers poured into my house to search. I was told that I was being charged for selling crystal meth while on federal bond and they had it all on tape. I lived down the street from my parent's, somehow one of my brothers saw all of the patrol cars in front of my house and called my parents. Next thing you know my parents are there trying to figure out what was going on. The mother of my kids was frantic as she held my one-year-old daughter, who didn't have the slightest clue to what was going on. My second son was next to me the entire time, too young to know what was going on. Once the detectives, officers, and agents finished searching my house, I was told to stand up. They told my family to say goodbye to me and that I would never raise my kids or be free again. My mom was crying and asked if she could pray for me before they took me. The officers looked at each other and nodded for her to go ahead. I put my head down and my mom began to pray over me, first in English, then right there, in front of all the officers, she began to speak in tongues. I believe it was a prophetic Word to my spirit because I felt the power of God so strong like I had never felt before. I was overwhelmed by what was happening and the very presence of God at the moment. I felt tears falling, even though I was fighting it. I didn't want the agents and detectives to see me breaking. Was I afraid of what was happening? Of course I was. Yet, this wasn't my first time arrested, it wasn't my first time facing felony charges. The tears were from something else. I felt Him. I felt God and I didn't understand it. I had quit living bad, I had quit making music. I had given it all up. So why was I being punished now! I didn't know what was happening in the living room at that moment, because in my heart I was having a conversation with God. I was pleading with Him on why this was happening. *Lord... really. After all of these years being a horrible person, and now that I'm doing good this happens to me. I got a job, I go to church, I treat my children good. I have given it all up!* Then I heard these words in my soul and I knew it was Him.

"You gave everything up except your life to me. That is all I wanted."

It made my heart sink and I could no longer hold back my tears. I snapped out of it and my mom had stopped praying. They were all hugging me. Finally, my little son was lifted up to me and he hugged me and I kissed him, telling him I love him and I will always love him. Next, my baby girl was lifted up to me and I kissed her.

"I love you mija, daddy loves you. I always will."

Then I was taken away and driven to the Sacramento County Jail and booked. I knew I was in big trouble. It didn't take me long to figure out what happened on that day in December. I was set up by someone I trusted. Because of my RICO charges in San Francisco I was immediately put into isolation.

I looked around my cell and couldn't believe that once again I was arrested. Why do I keep doing this? Why can't I just stop doing the things I do? When one is out in the free world, we fill it up with noise and clutter. I don't think we notice it until it's all ripped away from you. Then when it happens you realize that you hadn't thought or talked with yourself in a very long time. Life is filled with television, lunches, dinners, phone conversations, hanging out, music always playing and video games. Even reading books can stop you from talking to yourself. We fill our lives up with so many activities from the second we wake up until we fall asleep. This can go on for years. If you are on a long drive and listening to music and singing along. That is not spending time alone. You are still preoccupying your mind by blanking out and singing the lyrics. This was exactly what I had been doing for years. So for the very first time, I was forced to face myself. I walked over to the sink and looked into the shiny metal mirror. I realized that I didn't know me anymore. I didn't know this person that was looking back at me, and I didn't like who I saw. How stupid can I be? I just sat on my bunk in silence. I don't know how long I did this. It could have been twenty minutes or five hours. Time meant nothing in isolation. All was completely quiet as I sat there thinking back of my entire life.

I don't know the year it happened, but I'm pretty sure it happened a few years before I was born. One of my uncles, tio Juan accepted Jesus Christ as his Lord and Savior. Our family was Catholic, at least that's what we were told. Many times a Mexican family will say they are Catholic only because they grew up in it. So when my tio Juan came back to share about Jesus with my uncles, aunts, and grandparents, he was ridiculed and rejected. He wouldn't give up and continued to learn about Jesus through reading his bible and felt compelled to share it with the family. Finally, over time my beautiful grandmother opened her heart to the Lord Jesus and accepted Him. So did some of the rest of the family, and finally my grandfather. All of this happened in Texas, where my mother is from. Over time the gospel was shared with the rest of the family that was living in California and my mom accepted Jesus into her heart. I was five years old when this happened. I don't have any memories of my mom not being a believer. From that moment on my mom took me to every church service she attended. The thing that many people don't understand, is that Jesus is contagious. He is a magnet that does not need marketing or promotion. All He needs is for people to follow Him completely and be a living example. That is all it takes and revival will happen in your family, in your community, and in your city. The book of Acts is a perfect blueprint of what it should look like. There is something so pure and raw about the words of Jesus in this verse.

"And I, if I am lifted up from the earth, will draw all peoples to Myself." John 12:32

This is exactly what happened with the huge majority of my family. Within a few years, my dad's side of the family also accepted Jesus Christ. So many of my uncles were delivered from alcoholism during my childhood. Long gone were the days of my dad and uncles sitting around drinking alcohol. It was replaced by my uncles that knew how to play guitar worshipping God in the living room each time they visited each other. This was a normal thing for me. To see them in prayer and talking about Jesus. One of my uncles began pastoring a church and we all attended. Another uncle would lead worship with his amazing ability to play music. In seeing my dad accept Christ and completely change, I never had a problem in believing in God. My dad never 'acted' Christian in front of others, or during Sunday service. He was a different man, a different father. I could write an entirely different book on the beautiful things I witnessed in growing up in a predominately Christian family. Yet, even though I was taught better, and I had amazing examples of how true believers should live. I still wanted to do my own thing and live my life rebelliously.

I snapped back into the reality of sitting in my solitary cell without any idea of the time. I slid down to my knees.

"Lord, please help me. I want to accept you into my heart. I want to live a new life. I believe that you died on the cross and after three days you rose again. I repent of my sins and will believe in you for the rest of my life."

I waited after praying this prayer. One minute passed and nothing happened. I expected something magical or supernatural. I waited for joy to pour into my heart, or for the prison door to open with an officer saying 'you are free to go'. I didn't know what to expect but I expected something to happen, something to change. I continued waiting as I stayed kneeling on the concrete floor. Nothing was happening and for the first time in my life, I knew God had left me. It is hard to describe because I can't say I knew God was ever with me. Yet this absence, this complete feeling of floating with nothing underneath me or around me overwhelmed me. Suddenly I knew what life felt like completely void of God. It sucked the air out of me and caused me to tremble. I got up and laid on my bed. I felt an overwhelming horror that God was finally finished with me. Up to this point, no matter how much sin I was involved in, I never felt far from God. At times when I needed Him, all I had to do was pray and He would always answer. Even at times of being pulled over with drugs in my car, I would pray for God to protect me and sure enough the drugs wouldn't be found. I had hurt so many people and destroyed so much around me. Surely it was justice that I would be in this place and He would finally wash His hands of me. So many sermons I had heard that said Jesus was knocking on the door of my heart. Just waiting for us to accept Him in. What nobody ever told me was what happens when He is no longer knocking on the door. I thought I was going to hyperventilate.

"Jesus! Don't leave me. I'm sorry! I know you've left me to rot here. I know I don't deserve for you to forgive me!" The minutes then hours passed by and the empty void feeling never left. I repented over and over and over that entire first day. When a sheriff came to give me my dinner tray I asked him if there was any way I could get a bible. He said I had to request one from the chaplain. When he came back to pick up my food tray I handed him the request completely filled out. The next day I woke up with the same feeling that God had abandoned me. I still repented all day long hoping something would change. I felt nothing.

Each day that passed was a day of praying and repenting. Every time I saw the sheriff I would ask him if I had gotten any response yet from the chaplain for a bible. Each time I asked, he said that he hadn't heard anything back. After a few days, I received an answer from the chaplain stating that he had no more Bibles to give. He was sorry but explained that any bibles he had were from donations only, so he wouldn't have any until more were donated. A few hours later the same sheriff came to my cell and knocked so I would come to the door. I walked over, and he said,

"Look at what I found in a holding cell."

It was a paperback bible. I felt like a starving man finally given food. He opened my door slot and gave it to me. I thanked him repeatedly and he smiled and nodded his head. I immediately went to Genesis chapter one verse one and began reading. Each waking moment I was reading the Bible, reaching, yearning to feel the presence of God again. I had repented, I had pleaded, I had cried out to Him. My heart was broken and I felt like my soul was shattered. Not because of the jail cell, but because He no longer wanted me.

Six days had now passed and each day was the same. I was going to live this in this world, in this life with the complete utter rejection from God. I thought, 'this is my punishment.' It was now the seventh day, one full week since the day I was arrested. I was preparing to begin repenting again. Maybe this time He would hear me. Maybe this time He would have mercy on me. Surely He is a merciful God. Surely He couldn't ignore me forever. I got on my knees once again and couldn't even find the words anymore. I began to weep as I had never wept before. Then a thought popped into my head, an idea. *When I was arrested I didn't fight the police. I simply surrendered to them. And once I surrendered, I no longer had a say so on where I would go. I just had to go wherever the detectives took me. I was handcuffed and completely helpless.* I stopped sobbing and opened my eyes. I sat on my bunk and looked up. I began talking to God.

"Lord, I think I know what you want. And I am ready to give it to you. I don't accept You, I surrender to You. I completely surrender to You. My life is no longer mine, it is yours. You changed my dad in an instant, I saw it. Change me the same way you changed Him. I want to live for you with every breath I have until the day I die. I don't want to be a fake Christian, so please don't teach me how to only act good on the outside. I want you to change who I am on the inside. I will serve you all the days of my life...."

I stopped talking and sat there silently. Then I felt the weight come off of my shoulders. The weight of violence, wrath, and hate. The weight of being 'Dyno' and all that came with it. It was years and years of pain floating up and away from me. I felt a peace come over me as I had never felt before in my life. I felt Him, in the cell. Here with me!

"He's here! He's here!"

He didn't reject me, he didn't disown me.

He loved me and forgave me. I didn't deserve His love or His forgiveness, yet He poured it on me. That was the day that I became a new creation. He took out my heart of stone and put in a heart of flesh. Every plan the enemy had for me was broken.

After that moment, my perspective of the world was different. The way I thought about things was different. Don't get me wrong, there was still so much more to learn and mature in the things of God that to this day I am still learning. But I knew I was a new person, there was no doubt in my heart about that.

A few days later it was time for my court date. I wore shackles on my ankles with a chain that connected to another chain that was around my waist with handcuffs to keep my hands by my sides. I was transported next door to the federal building in downtown Sacramento. As I walked in I could see my parents and my family sitting there. I looked toward them and sat down in front of the judge. My appointed lawyer who had talked with me during a visit began to speak. I hardly understood anything that was being said as my lawyer, the federal prosecutor and the judge spoke. One thing I did hear loud and clear was the time my charges carried.

"We are charging David Rocha with

felonies that are a minimum mandatory of twenty-three years to life."

Did I just hear that correctly? I looked to my lawyer and she tried to argue the point. She was quickly denied any more time to speak and just like that, my court date was over for the day with another date mentioned for a continuance. I went numb. I knew I wasn't an innocent angel, but twenty-three years to life?... How can that be correct? Before I was able to gather my wits I was quickly taken back to the holding cell where I was in the back of the courtroom. I had to sit and wait most of the day as they took inmate after inmate to face the judge.

As soon as I was walked out my lawyer walked into the lobby with my family. They also heard what the judge had said and had a ton of questions.

"What happens now?" my mom asked.

"What do they mean twenty-three years to life?" asked my brother

"Can we bail him out?" asked someone else.

My lawyer was overwhelmed with the questions. She explained that I was denied bail and I would have to remain in custody until the next hearing.

My brother asked again, "What do they mean twenty-three years to life?"

She looked at my brother and my family and said, "Look... I'm sorry. I can't help him. They have him on videotape... Not even God can help him."

When she said that, my family got very quiet. *Did they just hear her right? Did she just say that not even God could help David?*

My brother Angel looked at her straight in the face. "You'll remember that when all of this is done." My family was almost joyful when the attorney said this. They knew that anytime someone challenged God throughout the Bible, that God always... always... always moved on behalf of His people. My family also knew that by her proclaiming that, in a federal building that represented such a mighty nation. That God was about to say, "Stand still for the fight is not yours, but Mine."

When I finally got back to my unit that evening I was allowed an hour in the solitary unit outside of my cell. I made a beeline for the phone and called home. By that time my parents were back home in Tracy, Angel was called on a three-way call.

"I don't know what to do," I said. "They can't be serious. There is no way I could ever get out of this. By the time I'm out, my kids will be grown. That's it! My life is over. I will never be free with you all."

Angel began to speak and explain to me

what happened in the lobby. It didn't make me feel any better knowing that my lawyer didn't think I had a chance. After Angel heard me venting and worrying for a few minutes he began to speak.

"David... I don't know what is going to happen. But I will say this to you with confidence. You are not going to do twenty-three years. God is going to move someway, somehow. Just watch and see what He does. Pray, believe and be strong."

I talked for a few more minutes before I hung up the phone. I had a horrible sinking feeling in my gut. But talking with them brought some light into this dark place. If they believed that God was going to do something, then I should also believe. This is where I began to learn to not determine my situation by what I saw around me. I was surrounded by concrete and metal, yet I would learn that God is stronger than any metal, any building and certainly any plan of the enemy. It was here that I would learn that God truly has the keys to every door. He opens doors and He shuts them at His will. I had no idea what was in store for me. But as I laid down to sleep I replayed in my mind the words of my lawyer to my family. *Not even God can help him.* I was afraid of what lay ahead of me. *What would my kids do without me? Would they forget about me? What would my parents and brothers do if I was going to serve a long sentence?* So

51

many questions with no answers. But one thing I did know. In my isolated cell, I was finally free. *Thank you, Jesus. I am free.*

4

45 DAYS OF LIGHT

45 Days of Light

After being in the same cell for a week, I was classified to be on the 8th floor which was solitary confinement. This floor was for those that were considered violent, dangerous or shot-callers. I did not understand why I was being put into solitary. I instantly filled out a request form to be moved out of solitary and to be put into general population. I also filled out another complaint form because my light in my cell wouldn't shut off. Each cell had a button on the side of the light fixture that had three modes. One was a low light setting so I can sleep, then a medium setting, and finally a full-on bright light that felt like the sun itself was in my room.

My cell light was stuck in this mode and wouldn't change. I continued to read my bible starting from the beginning. Federal court takes months between court dates, this was something I was going to learn as the days would slowly pass. First one week passed, then another. I still had not heard a response about my light or about my request to be put into general population. It was getting very hard to sleep with my cell so brightly lit so I would wake up and stay awake with no sleep pattern or sense of an internal clock. I tried to make the best of it when I would wake up by reading my bible, prayer and writing letters. As each week passed I would send out a complaint about hopefully moving to the general population and also repairing of my light in my cell. I began to learn how things operated in solitary by talking with others in my pod. I learned how inmates would make a long string out of their sheets or socks with a tightly folded paper at the end to act as a weight. Then they could send this out of the bottom of their cells toward another cell, all while the other inmate would shoot out his line until the two strings would tangle up and either of the inmates could pull the string into his cell and attach whatever he wanted, to send to the other cell. Once it was attached, the other inmate could just pull the string and back into his cell. Magazines, letters, commissary could be shared in this way between cells all along the pod. It was called fishing. I also learned how hot water could be passed from someone having their hour out in the pod to an inmate inside their cell. You could use a folded potato chip bag and stick it through the crack of the door at a slight angle. Then the inmate that was having his hour pod time would pour a cup of hot water into the folded potato chip bag and the person inside the cell would have a cup at the bottom of the bag inside of his cell as the water poured into his cup. This was a great way if you wanted to have hot water for coffee or a ramen soup. When I was tired of reading I would lay on my bunk and look out of my tinted window. I could see downtown Sacramento below as people and cars went about their business. Life does not stop and I wondered if I would ever know what it would feel like to be driving through streets again. The closest thing I can compare it to is if you passed away, and instead of burying you, you'd be put into a glass coffin and leaned against a wall in the living room of your house. That way you could see the ones you love living their lives, but you were unable to communicate or join them. You could scream out but they wouldn't hear you. Life just moved on. I began to drift off into my thoughts.

When I was in high school I remember rap

55

music was very popular. In the beginning, rap music was out of New York and a handful of rap artists from Los Angeles. The music was enticing and nice to listen to. Those of us that had cars would try to get the biggest sound systems in our trunk so the bass would make your chest rattle. I grew up going to Lowrider car shows and enjoyed the lowrider scene. Being in the church was boring to me. I wanted to be out and about with my friends. I wanted to cruise and meet girls. I also knew there was a darker world with gangs. Growing up in Tracy, our newspaper always had articles of the riots, stabbing, and fights that were happening at D.V.I. state prison that was just outside of Tracy. This enticed my friends and me. Once in a while, someone would be released from state prison and we would listen to them as they glamorized the life inside. It made us feel important and needed. I was told that people from my area were outnumbered in the state prison and they needed soldiers like us to help them. This embedded in our minds that there was a greater cause to fight. This along with learning about my history as a Mexican-American created a very twisted view of the world around me.

I was filled with pride and anger against anyone that opposed what I stood for. It didn't help when a big gang formed on the opposite side of

Tracy and they began jumping random people at school. What made it worse was after they jumped you, they would force you into their gang. I hung around a small group of guys that made a pact to stick together if this gang ever tried jumping any of us. We knew that it was a matter of time before they would come. Tracy was very small at the time and only had one high school. I refused to bow down to them no matter what. Then one day it happened. One of my best friends was walking home from school and they surrounded him and jumped him a few blocks away. We were still hanging around when he came to us completely enraged looking disheveled. I remember getting so angry that without thinking, a group of us piled into my car and drove back to where it happened. Most of them were gone but the two guys that were still there felt the wrath of what they did to my friend. This one incident completely split up the small town of Tracy to this day. My group formed into a gang that brought destruction to my small town for many years to come.

It was also during this time that I began to write poems about what I saw around me and how I was feeling about it. I had no intention of growing up to be in a gang, but the spiral had begun so quickly that it was not out of control. I never shared my poems with anyone, but it sure felt good to get my thoughts out on paper. One day a classmate that was sitting next to me saw me writing a poem in my book. He was a very known local DJ so I was embarrassed to show him my work. He insisted and I let him read one of the poems.

"Bro, you got to start rapping!" he said.

I laughed. "Come on man. Me rap? a Chicano? Rapping is for New York or Los Angeles. Who is going to listen to a Chicano from California, much less Tracy?"

"You can laugh all you want, but I think you got something here," he said.

I didn't say anything more to him but it stayed in my mind. Then I'd talk myself out of the idea and just continue writing my poems. Everything changed one day when I heard a song on a friends walkman.

"Who is this?" I said as I listened to a rapper with a style I had never heard of. It was so different. It wasn't breakbeats or a loop from a vinyl record. It was slow and had a rattling thick bassline throughout the entire song. It was like nothing I had ever heard.

"It's a rapper named Too $hort... He's from Oakland."

"Oakland! That's crazy," I said. I had always

thought rappers were from New York or Los Angeles and here was this local guy from Oakland. I was confused and couldn't imagine someone producing rap tracks that were so close to Tracy. Oakland was less than an hour away. He mentioned streets and landmarks that we all knew in his songs. He used slang that we all used. By the time a week passed by, every single person I came across was listening to Too $hort. He didn't even have a record deal and his cassette cover looked handmade. There was no photo of him on the front, just a small drawing, and the words Too $hort. His entire cassette was filled with original production, no sampling and that always evident thick rattling bassline. I was hooked. *If he can do it, and he's from northern California, then so can I.*

I began looking for instrumentals for songs that were usually on the flip side of the vinyl record. I didn't tell anymore that I began practicing my poems out loud to those instrumentals until I got better. In public, I was out gangbanging, but in my bedroom, I had aspirations on being the biggest Chicano rapper in the world. My poems became songs, and my lyrics talked about the things that were going on in local barrios. I used Chicano slang and would mention certain streets, and names of my friends. I also became friends with the DJ that originally encouraged me to rap. By the time I was seventeen I was deep into the gang, deep into becoming a rapper, and about to be a father to my oldest daughter. I had to grow up fast. I never reached my senior year in high school and was escorted off the grounds of the continuation school I attended. I tried looking for work and occasionally got hired, but I had so much pride and attitude that I would quit before giving the job a chance. I had my mind set on my aspiring music career as I continued to pursue a rap career. It wasn't long before a homeboy taught me how to sell marijuana. I remember arriving at his house one day and he had weed scattered all over his table and a small scale. Without hesitation he taught me all he knew about buying weed, weighing it and selling it. So there I was, eighteen years old with a new daughter, in a gang, rapping and selling weed. *I wish I could go back in time to talk to myself. I wonder if I would have listened? I doubt it.* I was getting on the fast track of life and the ride hadn't even begun to accelerate yet.

Being a follower of Jesus was very new to me, especially while incarcerated. My other two arrests I have had before this arrest was different. I would come in representing the cause I was taught to stand for. I didn't know what this would mean for me but I knew it wouldn't be good. I was told throughout the years that you could never leave the cause. It was more important than your own family, your own freedom and especially more important than your own life.

I heard a voice from my air vent above my sink and toilet that connected to the cell next to me.

"Hey homie, how's it going over there?" said the guy in my neighboring cell.

I stood up on my toilet so I could get closer to the vent. "I'm doing okay," I answered.

"Bro, I know you said you were requesting to go into general population. If they let you do that, just be careful bro. I shouldn't even be talking to you since you are no longer standing for the cause. If you are for real about Jesus then I respect it. I have a lot of Christians in my family."

I appreciated the times I would talk with my neighbor. It helped break up the time. These words he was telling me meant a lot because I knew that he held the keys for all the homies in the entire jail. Holding the keys meant that he was the one in charge, the shot caller for all the homies in the facility. No matter what floor, unit or pod, it all had to be approved by him. Many times we would talk for hours through the vent. He was fighting some serious charges also. Many times I would pray for him. Being a Christian was all new to me, yet here I was speaking the Word of God to the shot caller of the jail. I have always said that God is a master chess player. He is a strategic God that is always many steps ahead of you.

He continued talking. "I want you to be safe while you are in this jail bro. I can't straight out tell people to leave you alone. You know the rules man, we can't just leave this thing of ours. But what I can do is let them know that you are fighting a high profile federal case that could possibly bring repercussions for them from the OGs if they mess with you."

I didn't accept or decline the help he was offering. Matter of fact, to this day I don't think he was asking me if I wanted his help. Over the years I have thought of this situation that was very dangerous for me. First of all, I was just a regular guy from northern California. I grew up in Tracy and represented where I was from throughout my teen and adult years. But representing came at a cost that had ties all the way up the ladder in the underworld. Because of my rap career, it put me in a position to be in the presence of major players in the many cities in northern California and state prisons.

It was here that I first learned about making Cadillac drinks, which for us in Sac County Jail meant we would drop a Snickers bar into our hot coffee to sweeten it up. The chocolate and caramel would melt and it would make my coffee as smooth as a Cadillac. Sugar wasn't sold in commissary because many of the inmates would use it as an ingredient to make pruno. Pruno was a homemade prison wine made with fermented fruit and other ingredients. *I had never tasted coffee until Sacramento County Jail. To this day I still use chocolate in my coffee.*

After forty-five days I had completely read my paperback bible from front to back. As soon as I finished, I began reading it again from the beginning. I was still in my solitary cell and my light was still stuck on the brightest setting. I had forgotten what darkness felt like to sleep. The sheet they gave us was very thin, so even if I covered my head with the sheet, I could still see the bright light through my eyelids when I tried to sleep. Other times I tried to put wet toilet paper on top of the light so it could harden and create a cover over the light. I was told by the sheriffs to take it off or they would write me up. Believe it or not, this light problem created a fear of solitary confinement in me. I longed for a darkened cell to sleep in. One couldn't fathom torture by something so simple as a light, but trust me. It plays a huge psychological game on your mind.

I was laying down on my bunk reading

when I heard footsteps and keys rattling come into the pod. I put my book down when the steps got closer and closer to my cell. It was a sergeant and an officer. They opened my cell.

"David Rocha?" said the sergeant.

"Yes," I replied.

"I have your multiple requests to be moved into general population. I looked at your record and you have no violent offenses. To be honest I am worried because of your case in San Francisco. How do I know that If I consider letting you into the general population and you have prison gang ties because of your co-defendants that you will turn this jail upside down? The last thing I need is a gang war in my jail," He stared at me with an intense glare.

"Sir, I am fighting a case in San Francisco... but you will have no problem with me. I am stuck in this cell, my light won't shut off. I have been here for two months all by myself. I just want to fight my case and be around people. You will have no problems with me. You said so yourself that I have no violent offenses in the streets or in jail. Just give me a chance... please."

He looked at me for a few seconds and nodded. "I'll let you transfer to general population. But I will have my sheriffs watching you. If they sense anything weird, you'll be back here before you realize what happened. So get your stuff ready and I'll have you transferred after the count."

"Thank you. I appreciate it," I said.

He walked out of the cell, locked it and I could hear his footsteps as he walked away. *Wow, Thank you, Jesus. Thank You, Lord.*

"I told you it would be okay bro," said my neighbor.

"Yeah, thanks, man. I appreciate everything you've taught me and your company," I said.

"No problem. Just don't forget me and please say a prayer for me whenever you get a chance."

"Of course man, of course," I said.

So after almost two months in a brightly lit jail cell, I was transferred. Two sheriffs came into my cell and cuffed me. I grabbed my small box of property and was taken to an active pod. In every jail in northern California, a Chicano will either go into the active Southside pod or a Northside pod. This is usually classified by either the gang you claim or the city or neighborhood you are from. Because of my past affiliation, my pending San Francisco case and the town I was from, I was taken into an active Northern pod. I knew this was going to bring another set of problems. I figured it was better than being in solitary. When I left isolation, I prayed that

I would never have to be in complete isolation again. The experience left me with a fear of solitary confinement that I didn't know I had, not realizing it was something I would have to face head-on in the later months.

5

GANGS, SPREAD AND VISITS

I didn't care if it was an active gang pod I was going into, I was just happy to be out of solitary. I was walked to the pod and told which cell I would be staying in. I walked over and the door clicked open. When I walked in, my cellmate was already in the cell. Most might think it would be bothersome to be in a small cell with another person, but after solitary I enjoyed it. I quickly became friends with my celly and enjoyed the light fixture actually working when it was time to sleep. For the first time in two months, I actually rested well at night. It didn't matter that the mattress was so thin that my entire side of my body would go numb every few minutes and I had to keep turning all night.

Every single week I received visits from

family, especially my parents. They never missed a week which was a huge blessing. They had to drive an hour each way and I appreciated it. I learned to play Rummy 5000 which was a card game. I learned how to make prison spread where the main staple is Top Ramen noodles. Then you'd drain the water, add the flavoring and add other ingredients like pork rinds, chips, beef stick or anything else you wanted to add to it. Each day we were given pod time, which meant that after lunch the entire pod cell doors would pop open for a few hours before dinner. Everyone would come out with smiles as some watched television, took showers, used the payphones or sit at a table to talk or play card games. Because of my music career, I was recognized and respected. I was such a young believer that I didn't see an issue with sitting and joking with everyone during pod time, then when I was back in my cell I'd read and study my bible. Things were running smoothly for a few weeks.

Everything changed for me when I was reading my bible in my cell and came across a verse of the words of Jesus.

For whoever is ashamed of Me and My words, of him, the Son of Man will be ashamed when He comes in His own glory, and in His Father's, and of the holy angels. Luke 9:26

The verse hit me like a demolition ball. Jesus is saying that whoever is ashamed of Him, that in turn He will be ashamed of him back. Wow! Is this what I am doing? I study and pray each moment I am in my cell, but the second the cells open I go out into the pod and don't mention God. I didn't think anything was wrong with that. I wasn't out in the pod talking or acting the way I would of before surrendering to Jesus. Yet why did I feel a conviction in my heart? I realized that even though the Lord had changed me, I wasn't sharing it. The Gospel means the Good News, yet here I was keeping it to myself. The pod was full of men that needed Jesus, they needed forgiveness, they needed a new heart. Who was I to hide Jesus under a table? He is the light, and that light should shine brightly no matter where we are. And what place needs more light than a jail full of lost men? I had a choice to make. Was I going to go with the flow of an active gang pod? Or was I going to stand for Jesus regardless of the possible consequence?

The next day after lunch I knew it was just a matter of time before the doors would pop open for pod time. My heart felt like it was going to explode as the minutes passed. *Lord, I stand for you no matter what. Please protect me and give me wisdom.* A few minutes later all of the doors popped open and everyone came out of their cells. It was a regular routine for everyone else. Some ran to the phones, others to the showers, some to the television and others to the tables to hang out. I hesitated to step out, took a deep breath and grabbed my bible. I walked out of my cell and held my bible close to my side. Most didn't notice as they nodded their heads to me as I walked down the stairs and to a table. I sat down on the table, looked around and place my bible right in front of me. It seemed like nobody noticed. So far so good. I opened the Bible to the place I was reading in the cell and began reading. I know this isn't what happened, but to me, it felt like the movie 'The Matrix'. I felt everything completely stop and only I was moving. It didn't take more than two minutes before someone came to see what I was doing.

"What are you doing bro?" someone asked.

"Just studying. I was reading in my cell when the doors popped. So I just figured I'd read out here," I answered.

He just looked at me for a few seconds, then said. "Can I join you?"

I looked at him, not knowing if he was being serious. He sat down next to me and waited for me to read. After a few minutes, someone else came and sat down. Before I knew it I had a handful of guys sitting around as we talked about God. It was not what I expected at all. On this first day of coming out with my Bible in hand, it wasn't a problem. Many people in jail read the Bible. It wasn't anything out of the norm. Reading the Bible is what many do when incarcerated, especially before being sentenced. After a few days of me doing this, it began to be a problem. Nothing was said to me, but as the weeks went by I noticed tension against me. I was becoming bolder for Christ as other active gang members would sit with me to read the bible and discuss things about the Lord. Each time I used the phone I never stood with my back to everyone. Some of the homies began ignoring me. I think they were confused because of the high profile case I was involved with, plus I was positive the shot caller that was on the 8th-floor solitary was looking out for me. I will never know for sure why nothing happened. Being in an active pod meant that everyone in that pod was obligated to be active. One thing I do know is that the Lord kept me and protected me.

A few weeks later, the jail was getting full and they had to open an overflow pod on a different floor. I was one of the few chosen and was transferred along with about ten others to a nearly empty pod. By this time the tension was heavy and I knew it was leading to something bad. I thanked

God as we all came into the pod. There were only a few of us, so we were all allowed our own cell. I was asked by the sheriff if I wanted to be a trustee along with another inmate. This was an amazing opportunity. A trustee never has his cell door locked. A trustee's job is to mop the floors, clean the showers, serve breakfast, lunch, and dinner and pretty much be a janitor for the pod. This meant that I could use the phone anytime I needed and take showers anytime I wanted to. I thanked God for giving me favor. While everyone else was locked in their cells until after lunchtime, I was given free rein to go in and out of my cell all day with the other trustee. This put me in an amazing opportunity to talk to the other inmates through their doors when they were locked down. Of course, it was too perfect to last. Each week that passed, more of the cells began to fill up. Before I knew it, most of the cells were full and I no longer had a single cell. I didn't mind having a cellmate. Our door was never locked so we were never cramped up in the cell together. I had continued giving Bible studies since day one of arriving in the empty pod that was now full. Anytime you get a jail pod full of men, there will always be tension. Even though the pod was an overflow pod, it was still considered an active pod.

No matter if you were a northerner, blood or whatever you claimed.

It had now been over a year since my first arrest. My court dates were so far apart that months would go by before I had another court date. Things weren't looking good on my behalf. The Prosecutor was trying to sentence me under the career criminal law, which could be a minimum mandatory sentence of twenty-three years.

(Career Offenders are persons who commit a crime of violence or drug trafficking crime after two prior felony convictions for those crimes. To implement the provisions of 28 U.S.C. § 994(h), the sentencing guidelines assign all career offenders to Criminal History Category VI and to offense levels based on the statutory maximum penalty of the offense of conviction.)

My lawyer was doing all she could to fight against the career criminal statute. I tried to make my time pass easier by giving Bible studies to the different men that would come and go. I began to feel myself losing hope in ever being released with a short sentence. Life in jail became my norm and my life outside began to fade away. The one goal I had was to get back to the family I had. If this was a race, then they were the prize at the end. I had to see my youngest daughter walk for the first time through the glass in the visiting room. I heard her first words through a collect call on the payphone. I was watching my children grow up through the visiting room double-paned window as I felt my involvement in their lives slipping away as the months passed. My oldest daughter who was now in high school didn't have her father around in the most crucial time for a growing teenager. My sons were growing up without a dad to be an example for them. I thank God for my dad and my brothers for stepping in and being that father figure for them. My second daughter felt so far away from me. I wondered if they would remember me as the years passed. Would my parents still be around when I would walk out of prison? These thoughts haunted me.

Things took a turn for the worse one day when the guy holding the keys of the pod came to talk to me. When someone holds the keys, it means he runs the pod. Usually by permission given to him from people higher up in the gang that is on other floors or pods in the jail. Many that haven't been to jail would believe that it would be impossible for communication to happen between jail pods, floors and even other facilities and prisons across the state. This is far from the truth. Word travels fast throughout the prison and jail systems. Someone, somewhere knows exactly who is running each jail, each floor, and each pod.

"David, I need to talk to you," said the shot caller.

"What's going on?" I asked.

"First of all, I shouldn't even be telling you this... but, you need to roll it up," he said as he looked directly at me. To 'roll it up' meant to get your property and hit the buzzer in your cell that is there only for emergencies. Then tell the authorities that you can't be in that pod and that you need to be in protective custody. This is a touchy subject because it is looked down on among inmates, and is something that will follow you throughout your entire time in prison and possibly when you get released.

I looked at him and said, "I'm not leaving this pod." He shook his head and I walked away from his cell. I knew the repercussions that could happen, yet I felt stuck. Nobody knew better than me how serious the situation was. I didn't want to go back to solitary, I was unwilling to 'roll it up' and I knew I was in an active pod. I had a great job as a trustee in a cell that was never locked. I decided that I would stick it out and remain in the pod. I had a good relationship with most of the inmates and the sheriffs trusted me as a worker. One thing I find interesting about many Christians in the free world compared to Christians that are incarcerated is the level of commitment to Jesus. I cannot speak for all institutions or all situations, but for me to follow Christ it had to be a commitment to the point of death. Nothing less would work. In prison, we learn to see right through people. If there is no confidence or grit then the wolves will eat you right up. There was no way I could have played the 'Christian' in the place I was at. I never considered myself a coward before Christ, so how could I be a coward now, in Christ. I didn't want anything to happen, and of course, I had fear. I am in no way saying that I was a superhero. By this time in my walk in Christ, I didn't know a whole lot, but I did trust in God. Either He would protect me or He wouldn't. Regardless I was going to stand for Jesus no matter what. It was a decision I engraved into my heart and mind. In the same way, I was willing to die for the cause, how much more should I stand for Jesus. I continued to give my bible studies when the men would come out for their pod time. A few days passed with no incident other than looks from the homies. My 'antenna' was always on high alert without showing it, as I continued to do my regular job and program.

One day during pod time I decided to go into my cell to rest. I had been cleaning the showers and mopping the pod along with my celly since the morning. So, by the time the rest of the inmates were given their pod time, I was tired. Even though having a cell that was never locked was a big benefit, there was one downfall. Which was the fact that anyone could also come into our cell. Even though this was a concern, I would assure myself that nobody would ever come into our cell unannounced. To an inmate, your cell is your house. The same disrespect you would feel if someone would just open your front door and walk in was the same if you would walk into someone's cell. To top it off, my celly was both feared and respected. So to come into our cell was not only a disrespect to me, but also to my celly.

I was reading on my top bunk and began to feel sleepy. I decided to shut my eyes for a few minutes and lay my head back. I began to doze off as I heard the pod full of conversations, television, and men walking up and down the stairs to the second tier. After a few minutes, I was startled. I quickly opened my eyes and looked around. I didn't understand why I was awakened so quickly but I instantly sat up. Now in looking back, I truly believe it was the Holy Spirit that quickened me to wake up. A few seconds later my cell door is pulled wide open and three men rush toward me. I had to think quickly because I was sitting with my legs dangling off of the bunk. If these men would have gotten a hold of my ankles, they could have pulled me down which could have cracked my skull on the way down. Adrenaline kicked in and I snapped into survival mode. I quickly assessed the situation and saw that the three guys were smaller than me. As long as more wouldn't come into the cell, I was ready to fight all three men. I quickly balled up my fist to hit the closest guy to me, then time stopped. I don't know any other way to explain it. But within the millisecond of all that was happening. Them coming into the cell. Me jumping off of my bunk. The three men rushing toward me and my fist balling up to hit the first guy. It was like God hit a pause button just to speak to me. It wasn't an audible loud voice, but nevertheless, it was a voice with authority. *'Why are you going to fight? If I didn't fight them when they beat me, who do you think you are? This isn't you anymore'.* At that moment, I released my tight fist as I felt punches and kicks. I lifted up my arms to protect my face.

I heard a loud explosive voice. "Hey! Hey! What are you doing!" yelled my celly. He was dead asleep and awoke in a fury. The moment he stood up the three guys all ran out of our cell. My celly followed after them. I could hear him yelling right outside of the cell.

"Who wants some? I'll take any of you on! What makes you think you can come into my house!" he yelled as they all stepped away from him.

One of them spoke up. "No disrespect to you bro, but David has to roll it up!"

"What do you mean no disrespect to me! You already disrespected me when you came into my cell!" he said.

"Okay, Okay! We are sorry. Send David outside then... so we can finish this," Said one of the homies.

I was up and washing my face when he walked back into the cell.

"Hey, are you okay David?"

"Yeah, I'm good. Just got a few hits to the head."

"Well, they aren't coming into here again. Just stay in the cell."

"No, I can't do that. I'm going to go outside. I don't want to drag you into this," I said as I looked at him.

"David, you don't need to do this. Just stay in the cell for now. I won't stop you bro, but I don't think you should go out there."

I looked at him and looked outside. There was a crowd of about twelve homies waiting to see what was going to happen. I then opened my door and stood outside my cell.

"David... you gotta roll it up!" said one of them aggressively. I saw them all coming closer.

"Hold on," I said. "I want to say something to each of you."

I couldn't understand it but I had their undivided attention. I was surprised they all didn't attack. I continued to speak. "I know that you all want me out of here. I get it, I know the rules. But God has blessed me with this job as a trustee and I'm not going to lose it. I know that when you are all together, everybody wants to act like you don't care about anything. When you go back to your cells and it's late at night, I know for a fact that you all pray to God for mercy on your cases that you are all fighting. Everyone here is fighting a case. I am here to tell you one thing. After what you just did to me, don't expect to have God do anything on your behalf. How do you expect God to answer your prayer after what you are doing right now to His servant? The Bible says that you cannot touch the Lord's anointed. I no longer stand for the cause... I was conflicted between God and you all. But, after today. I know where I stand. I stand for Jesus 100%."

I braced for the punches and kicks that I was about to get. I looked at each of them as they simply stared at me. I don't know if they were thinking about my words, or if they were in shock for the simple fact that I was speaking so boldly. The silence was broken up by the loudspeaker.

"Dinner time! Everybody! lock it in."

To this day I don't know if the sheriffs saw what was happening. The assault was in my cell, so I know they didn't see that. And there was so much movement in the pod that it could have looked like we were just talking. Besides the fact that the two sheriffs not only overlooked our pod but two others from where they sat. Within a few seconds, the crowd dispersed and everyone went back to their cells.

I didn't know what to think. I didn't know what to do. My celly and I walked outside of the pod to bring in the food cart. As was usual, one of the sheriffs came down and into the pod as the doors popped for everyone to come to get a tray and go back to their cells. First, the bottom tier formed a line first. Once the bottom tier had gotten their food tray, they let out the top tier. Each time I handed a tray to someone that was a part of the crowd against me, I would say, "God bless you." This caused each one to have a confused look on their face. The strangest thing to me was how I didn't feel rage, anger or hate. I actually felt sorry for them. This was so different for me. In the past, it would have gone down completely different. Somehow, someway, God had changed my heart.

Later on, that evening, while everyone was locked down for the night. I heard my name from the top tier. I looked up and saw that it was the shot caller. I walked up to his cell and saw him standing and looking out through his window.

"What are you doing, David? Why are you making this so difficult?" he said through the crack of the door.

"I'm not going to leave here. God blessed me with this job. You want me to roll it up? I am not going to do the rest of my time with that on my record. And someday I'll finish my sentence and I'll go back to Tracy. How am I going to share Jesus with them if they know I rolled it up? You know and I know that they won't respect me after that."

"I should have broken your jaw earlier," he said. I didn't say anything. "Next time, you are going to leave on a stretcher, David."

"I doubt it. I don't say that to disrespect you, bro. I know where you are coming from. I might be wrong, but I believe that the Lord is not going to give you another chance to hurt me. All-day I asked God why He allowed that to happen to me. It all makes sense to me now. He allowed it to happen for my sake. I still felt a bond with you guys up to this point, because it's all I stood for since I was a teenager. God wanted me to make up my mind who I stood with. So you know what... I thank you for what you guys did today."

"You are making a big mistake, David. The stuff you are teaching is poison to our cause." Then he looked at me and walked back to his bunk. Within two days after that, every single person that enforced his rules was removed from the pod. One of them was sentenced and sent to prison. Another got into a fight with another inmate and was sent to solitary. Still, another was released. There were other homies in the pod, but none of them were firestarters. Everyone noticed that the very guys that went into my cell were no longer there. I continued to give Bible studies every single day. None of the homies were allowed to sit at my table, and those that did were instantly jumped, yet I was never touched again. I would give Bible studies to blacks, whites, and Asians. Months passed and I continued to get my weekly visits from my family and friends. I didn't know what was in store for me in the future, but I knew that God was going to do this time with me.

6

GOD CHANGED
THE LAWS

The time in court was now winding down to either go to trial or plead guilty. My options for fighting the case was a joke. I was caught on video and audio selling crystal meth to a friend. Never in my wildest dreams did I think this friend of over a decade would be a paid informant. The only argument my lawyer had was to fight against the 'career criminal statute' which would put me at twenty-three years to life sentencing bracket. The leverage the prosecutor offered was to not 'career criminal' me if I pled guilty, not go to trial and take a lesser sentence. Basically I was at the mercy of the court.

Before I continue on, I need to explain how the Federal Courts operate when it comes to sentencing. In 1984 a sentencing guideline was created during the presidency of Ronald Reagan. Without being too technical, I will explain it in layman's terms to the best of my ability. One of the most controversial legacies of the Reagan administration was the war on drugs. This was the height of Pablo Escobar and many others that were smuggling cocaine into the United States. Places like Miami were operating like the wild west. Drug kingpins were rising everywhere, with executions running rampant. Street gangs had the public in terror in urban cities from New York to Los Angeles. People were in fear and looked to the President to fix America. This brought on the creation of strict anti-crime measures, including a sentencing guideline for federal judges that would be uniform throughout the fifty states. Parole for federal inmates was abolished and mandatory minimum sentences were brought on for weapons and drug cases. Before the sentencing guideline existed, a federal judge in California could give a defendant a three-year sentence, and in New York, a different federal judge could sentence a defendant twenty years for the same exact crime. President Reagan wanted to completely usher in unforgiving legislation to put away criminals once and for all. Federal judges could no longer give out sentences according to their own will. A guideline was created that looked very much like a multiplication table. On the left side of the chart going down was a crime, with different degrees of that crime from low to highest the further it went down. Across the top of the chart were months to sentence according to the criminal history of the person being sentenced. Beginning with a minimum amount of months and adding up the further it went to the right. In the years to come, these anti-crime measures would fill up federal prisons across the United States with non-violent drug offenders being put away for decades at a time. For years lawyers and judges have fought against these strict guidelines with no avail. The Federal Guidelines were law and nothing could budge them.

I saw no more reason to keep fighting the inevitable. I was going to go away for a very long time and I just had to accept that. My spirit was broken because of my family and my children. I realized how selfish I was, to do what I was doing out on the streets. There is a saying, 'Don't do the crime if you can't do the time.' Yet this leaves the family out of the equation. When a person lives a reckless life that sends them to prison, they fail to realize that the entire family will suffer. The children and family are never given the option or choice. Thousands of grandparents, parents and loved ones die before they see the incarcerated loved one free. Multitudes of children grow up with one less parent, or sometimes both parents absent during their most crucial years. Spouses have to learn how to maintain the family financially and walk about living life like a widow. Being the one incarcerated is like watching the entire family crumble, and no matter how much you scream and yell, the prison walls mute your every cry.

I told my family that I was going to tell my attorney that I would plead guilty. Everyone agreed that it was my only option. When she came to visit me, we talked about her meeting with the prosecutor to tell him that I decided to not go to trial. After a few weeks, my attorney came to visit me with a plea agreement in her hand. It stated that if I pled guilty, the prosecutor would not charge me under the criminal career statute and I would have to serve a 162-month sentence (13.5 years). I reluctantly shook my head and said okay. I felt defeated. She said she would get back to me with a court date to officially sign the agreement.

The days after that melted into each other. All I could think of was the court date where I would sign over a decade of my life to the Federal Courts. I felt like I was free-falling further and further away from my family. Hearing their voices over the phone felt like stabs to my heart. Seeing my mother and father in the visiting booth broke me as I saw the pain in their eyes. I tried to stay strong for them, but sometimes the tears fell anyway. I continued to study the Bible with men in the pod as usual. At night I would pray for God to wake me up from this nightmare. *What have I done, Lord? My children need me. I was so selfish... how could I have been so blind?*

A few days later I was called for a visit. I knew it would be my parents. They came every single week. I was excited to see that they had brought my aunt Benny. I called her Tia Benny. She was my dad's sister and very much a second mother to me. No matter what I did in my life, she loved me no matter what. Her loud laugh was contagious and her love for God was beautiful. She accepted Christ not too much longer after my dad. If there was ever a prayer warrior contest, I believe she would win hands down. There were times where she would fast and lock herself in her room for days at a time in prayer. She would receive prophetic words for those in her life. The power and love of God were clearly evident in her life. I recognized this even as a non-believer. She never hesitated to sit me down to talk to me about Jesus. I loved her so much that no matter how I was living, I'd always listen and nod my head. At times she would scold me like a child then tell me she loved me. I would always hug her and thank her for her words.

As they came into the visiting booth, they had to take turns talking to me through a phone hanging on the wall. She sat patiently as my mother talked with me first, then my dad. When it was her turn, she slowly sat on the stool and faced me. She smiled and greeted me.

"Hi, mijo... how are you doing?"

"I could be better tia," I answered.

"I came to tell you something." Her face became serious. I nodded, ready to receive whatever it was she wanted to tell me.

She continued. "Mijo, I was in prayer for you and the Lord gave me a vision... He is going to show your family and everyone that He is powerful and in control. That through you! Many will know that there is a God in heaven. He has a plan for you, and you will bring thousands to Him."

Upon hearing these words I began to cry. It was as if the Lord Himself was talking through her. *What did these words mean? Was God going to set me free? Was He going to open the gates for me to be released? How would I bring thousands to Him?*

At the same moment, I was thinking these things, my tia began praying for me so powerfully that I thought I would drop to the floor. She began speaking in tongues and the presence of God was overwhelming. I was now crying openly, my mom was crying, my dad was crying. We were having church service in the visiting booth. A few minutes later my visiting time was over. I thanked her for visiting me and I said goodbye to my parents. I walked back into the pod full of hope and life.

Sometimes when we get a Word from God, we can interpret it wrong. Then when it doesn't happen as we thought, we stop believing it was truly a Word from God. I was still a very new and young Christian. I was clouded by the 'now' instead of the big picture. When my tia told me that God was going to show my entire family that He was powerful and in control. I Interpreted it as God was going to open the doors of the jail and I wouldn't be sentenced to all of those years. That someway, somehow a miracle would happen and I'd be set free. Then everyone would know that God is powerful and in control. This was very confusing because my cousin Carlos came to visit me also during this time. He knew about my plea agreement and began to fast and pray for me. He wanted to share with me about the Word from the Lord that he received during his fasting.

"David, I have been fasting for days in prayer for you. I came to share with you His words. He said that you shouldn't worry about 13.5 years. That you will sign the plea agreement, but you will only do a little over five years in prison."

"Five years! What do you mean? God is going to release me from this place!" I said. I felt angry at him for speaking a five-year sentence into my life. I refused to receive it. I explained to him about my tia visiting me and the words she prophesied over my life. He didn't want to disagree out of respect.

"Cousin... I don't know anything about what she told you. All I know is that you are going to do a little over five years. He is going to prepare you in here. I didn't mean to come and make you angry. I thought you would be happy. Primo, you are not going to do the 13.5 years!"

"Carlos, that doesn't make any sense. I am about to sign a 13.5-year plea agreement."

Carlos shrugged his shoulders. "I don't know. All I know is what He showed me."

I tried to hide my anger as we continued our visit. I was grateful for the visit and didn't want to be disrespectful.

The day came for my court date. The marshals would come to the jail to pick up any federal inmates that were scheduled to appear in court. A chain would be placed around our waist that had two chains going down each leg with a shackle on each end and two chains at the side of the waist with handcuffs at the end. Then we would be taken down by elevator and put into a van. The Federal Court was across the street from the jail. After the short ride, we would be taken into the Federal building and taken up to the floor of the courtroom. Once there we would be placed into holding cells until it was time to face the judge. After some time, my name was called. The marshal came to my cell and walked me into the courtroom. I quickly glanced and saw my parents and family there. Words were exchanged between the judge, the prosecutor, and my attorney. My mind was in a haze as I tried to understand all of the legal terms being used. Finally, I was asked to plead. I pled guilty. Then I was asked to sign the plea agreement for a 13.5-year sentence. I guess my tia Benny and my cousin Carlos were both wrong. No doors opened for me, no five-year sentence. My name was signed on the agreement and that was it. According to the Federal sentencing guidelines, I was going to serve 13.5 years. Nothing more and nothing less. The guideline could not be budged. I was then given another court date to be formally sentenced. I was taken back to the holding cell until everyone else was finished with their court dates. We were all transported back to the

Sacramento County Jail. After all of these months of waiting, it was finally finished.

Weeks passed before my court date arrived. I still remember the day very clearly. I was up early because I knew that the marshals would come early to pick me up. I wanted to make sure I could shower and drink my coffee while reading the paper. When I walked out of my cell I didn't pay any attention to the Sacramento Bee as I made my way to the shower. Once I was finally ready, I made my coffee and made my way to get the paper from the table. When I saw the front page I nearly passed out. I could not believe what I was seeing. It was impossible. I had to sit down at one of the tables in the pod to get my composure. In big letters across the front page were the words, *Federal Guidelines found unconstitutional* by the Supreme Court. The day was January 13, 2005. After twenty-one years, the laws were changed on the day I was to be sentenced. This now gave more power to the judges to either go above or below the Federal Sentencing Guidelines. For the past two decades, a judge had to sentence the guilty defendant by the chart with no wiggle room. The marshals never came to pick me up that morning. After a few hours of not knowing what was happening, I was called for a visit with my attorney. As soon as she heard about the decision by the

Supreme Court, she immediately canceled my sentencing court appointment. From what I heard from her, every sentencing court session was canceled across the board that day. I was in awe. I remembered back when my attorney told my family on my first court date when she said: "Not even God can help him."

My parents had shown up to the court and soon found out that the court date was canceled. They got worried and instead came to the jail to see if they could visit me. I couldn't hold my excitement when I was called for a visit. My words were stumbling over each other as I shared with them all that I knew. We were all in complete awe. We shed tears and thanked God for His goodness and mercy. I explained to them that we weren't out of the woods yet. My lawyer still had to figure out if this could help me. She had a lot of studying to do with the big change. She had to now figure out how to reverse my plea agreement that I had already signed for 13.5 years. After a few days, I was given a new sentencing date which was to take place in March of 2005. I just knew that God's hand was stronger and bigger than the judges, the courts and the nation.

As time moved closer to my sentencing date, my attorney advised me that the new law could potentially backfire on me. Now that the judge had the right to go below or above the sentencing guidelines, ever since the new law came into effect, many judges were giving more time to defendants than the guidelines recommended. By this point, nothing she said worried me any longer. I knew that the Lord was with me and His will would be done.

I waited two months while the courts were drowning in sentencing motions over the new law. The days, visits from family and jail life felt like a blur. After a few weeks, my lawyer finally came to see me with a solid court date for sentencing. Two days before I stood in front of the judge, I decided to fast. I wanted to be spiritually and mentally on point. I prayed with my family over a visit and phone calls. It was hard to concentrate on any of my tasks as a trustee. Some people were coming back with more time due to the new law allowing the judge to go below or beyond the sentencing guidelines.

When the morning finally arrived for me to go to court, I was a bit nervous, yet overall I felt an overwhelming peace. I was now my third day of fasting and being in prayer. The marshals came to get everyone that had court that day. They chained us with shackles on our ankles, waist, and wrists and we were transported by van over to the building next door to the Sacramento County Jail. It was the Federal courthouse. We were taken into the back of the building that had a high wall and security gate that allowed us in and closed in behind us once we drove in. The van was full of other inmates. We were taken out and walked into an elevator made for inmates and told to face the back wall. Once we stopped at our floor we were guided to holding cells until it was time for our hearing. I made small talk with other inmates but my mind was somewhere else.

Before I knew it, I myself was standing in front of the judge. I quickly looked back and saw my entire family sitting. My lawyer leaned over.

"David, I usually never let my clients speak when the judge asks you if you have any words before he passes judgment. They usually make it worse for themselves. Yet for you, I believe you should speak... It's up to you."

I whispered back, "Yes, I want to speak."

"Ok, the judge will ask you if you have any words. That will be your cue."

My lawyer quickly began to bring up the new law and the new motion on why I should be reduced in the sentence I originally signed for. She was retracting my accepted sentence of 13.5 years. The moment my lawyer said this, the prosecutor went into a frenzy.

"Your honor, Why are we discussing this! Mr.

Rocha has already pled and agreed to 162 months and has already signed it. We are all here to simply formally sentence him," said the prosecutor.

The judge was fast with his words. Looking at the prosecutor he said, "Who's courtroom is this?"

The prosecutor hesitated... "It is yours, your honor." The judge nodded.

"Thank you for acknowledging that. So as I was saying, I would like to hear the motion."

My lawyer was then able to state the motion and reasons why my sentence should be reduced under the new law. The Judge didn't nod his head yes, or no. He just simply listened with the best poker face imaginable. Once the motion was read, he finally looked at me in acknowledgment.

"Mr. Rocha, before I sentence you, do you have anything you would like to say?"

"Yes, your honor," I said.

"Go ahead."

I looked back at my family then looked at my lawyer. She nodded for me to speak. "First, I want to thank you for this opportunity... I want to apologize to this court, to my community and to my family for breaking the law. By my actions, I have brought heartbreak to my family and my children. I know that you must hear this daily, your honor. But I have surrendered my life to Jesus Christ. I completely submit myself to whatever sentence you choose to give to me as a payment to society for my wrongs. I know and understand that serving this sentence is paying back society, but I want you to know that as a Christian, I will continue to pay back society once I am released for the rest of my life. To stop this lifestyle by telling people about Jesus Christ. To reach out to my community to help them get out of this lifestyle...."

I stopped speaking and the judge stared at me. For me, it felt like hours, but it was probably more like ten seconds. "Are you done speaking, Mr. Rocha?"

I nodded yes.

"Ok, thank you for speaking... You are correct Mr. Rocha. I do hear it every day in my courtroom that an inmate has found God.

I looked down and thought to myself. 'I knew it! He didn't believe me and he just said that everyone says that to him. I knew it! I should have kept my mouth shut. Lord, please help me.'

The judge began to speak again. "So many come into my courtroom talking about change, yet, for some reason, I believe you. I am reducing your sentence to 90 months."

The prosecutor looked toward me in disgust and I was quickly taken back to a holding cell. It was a complete act of God. From 13.5 years to 7.5 years.

After a few hours, I was taken back to the county jail and was visited by my family. We cried tears of joy and sadness because there were still many years I would be away from home. The worst part of the entire day was calling my oldest daughter to tell her the news that I wouldn't be around for the next few years. A young girl just beginning her teenage years, the time she needs her father the most, and I was going away. I had talked to her about high school graduation since she was a child, and I was going to miss it.

I waited three months for the marshals to come get me for transportation to prison. I continued to live in the same active pod during my entire wait. I continued to give bible studies each and every day. Much of the tension was still there due to the shot-caller frustrated with the fact that I refused to roll it up and go to protective custody. Yet, for reasons I didn't know about, nothing was being done to remove me from the pod. For security reasons, inmates are never told when they will be picked up, nor what prison you are going to. Being a federal inmate means they can send you to any prison within the fifty states.

I was awakened by my speaker in my cell. "Rocha, come to the control tower."

"Ok," I answered half asleep. I quickly made my way over to the tower.

The officer opened the door. "Marshals are coming to get you in fifteen minutes. Get all your property and call your family to come to get it. You can't take it with you. You can't take anything with you. Also, tradition is that every trustee chooses who takes the job... So who do you want to take your job?"

I thought for a few seconds and said the shot-callers name.

"Ok, you got it. I'll let him know so he can move into your cell."

I quickly walked back to my cell so I could put my property in a box for my family. I could hear the shot-callers intercom in his cell and his door popped open. He walked out with a confused look on his face. He slowly walked over.

"You leaving now?" he asked.

"Yeah, marshals are coming to get me and the sheriff said I could decide on who would get my job... I told him that you'd be a good worker."

David, why would you do that? After all the problems I've given to you."

I looked at him and said, "I know that you are fighting a big case that might put you away for life.

I figure that with all of that stress, you'd appreciate being out and about here while you fight your case."

He looked down feeling ashamed. "David, I'm really sorry man. I wish I was man enough to do what you are doing and living for God. No matter where you go, don't change. Keep doing what you are doing. I respect you." Then he reached over and hugged me.

I reached down for my box. By this time everyone was awake and looking out of their cells. I yelled out 'bye' to everyone and left the pod for the last time. I handed my property box to the sheriff and stood in line for the marshals to transport me. Once we left the jail I quickly found out that I was being taken to Santa Rita County jail to face my original judge in San Francisco. I was arrested while on Federal bond and due that that, I would have to face the judge to be sentenced for committing a crime while on bond. Up to this point, Sacramento County jail was easy time, I just didn't know it yet.

7

SOLITARY
CONFINEMENT

As I approached the Santa Rita Jail in the very prosperous city of Dublin California, it was a complete contrast to its surroundings. The jail was hidden behind high-end restaurants, beautiful shopping centers, auto dealerships and an Imax Theater surrounded by a massive food court with no homelessness, gangs or drug addicts in sight. Most consumers haven't the slightest idea that within a few yards, sits one of the biggest county jails in the country. The jail sits on 113 acres and laid out in a modern-looking prison-style facility. It stretches across a one half-mile-long stretch and a quarter-mile wide plot. The entire facility has eighteen separate, self-contained housing units and a core building that contains the central booking, release, and administration along with a service building for laundry, commissary, kitchen, and warehouse. It is considered a mega-jail and holds 4,000 inmates at a time.

Once we arrived we were taken straight to booking. Each time an individual is taken to a new facility, you are booked all over again for the records of that specific jail. Fingerprints, photos of tattoos and classifying are normal protocol. We were told to stand in line and wait as each of us was booked. I was third in line as we all stood up against a wall. When my time was up I slowly walked up to the officer. They asked my name and compared it to their paperwork. I gave my fingerprints and they took a photo of me. The last part of the booking was photos of any tattoos I had.

"We need to take a photo of each tattoo you have," said the sheriff.

"No problem," I said, knowing to show my tattoos on my hand and forearm. Then I lifted up my sleeve to show the tattoo on my left back-arm that said, 'Sir Dyno'. The moment the officer saw the tattoo he instantly ordered the other inmates to put their faces to the wall.

"Get your face to the wall!" he yelled out to me. I heard them talking and calling a superior officer on their radio. I was instantly separated from the rest of the group and put into a solitary holding cell. I had no idea what was going on, but apparently they knew exactly who I was. I was given clothes to change into and was told to wait.

I sat in the cell for what felt like two or three hours before an officer came to open the cell door. I was given a thin sheet, hands cuffed behind me and told to follow him. It was a Friday night and the jail corridor was silent. I could hear the jingling of his keys and our shoes as we walked down the longest hall I had ever seen. Finally, when we reached our destination, we approached a huge solid door that opened with the sound of metal on metal. We walked in and soon found ourselves in front of another similar door. I felt as if I had fallen into a deep pit with the known world slipping away. 'what is this place?' Deeper and deeper, door after door. This must literally be the abyss, a place of nothingness, a very tangible place of forgetfulness. My skin crawled at the thought that I would never leave this place alive.

We reached our destination as I saw a control tower with two officers sitting inside of it. They both looked down toward me as I was taken into one of the pods. I was walked to one of the cell doors, it was opened and I was told to step in and walk all the way to the bunk facing the wall. Once I was in the door was shut behind me. I was then told to walk backward and a slot was opened where I could stick out my hands. The handcuffs were taken off and the metal slot door was slammed shut.

I looked around the cell and realized it was very similar to my cell in Sacramento. One thin mattress, no cellmate and the typical sink with a built-in toilet. I looked into the shiny metal that was supposed to be a mirror, I could hardly make out my reflection. Once the officer walked out of the pod, I could hear many of the men in the other cells begin to talk. I was told that I was in complete segregation, solitary confinement. I sat back in my bunk and the reality of solitary caused my heart to sink deeper into despair. The thoughts of those forty-five days with the light switch broken came rushing back. An air vent on the wall was loudly blowing cold air into the cell. I tried to cover myself with the thin sheet, but it did no good in keeping me warm. I was given no pillow, no issue of a toothbrush, toothpaste, pencil, envelope or stamp. All I had was a thin sheet and a towel. I rolled the towel up and used it as a pillow. I laid down and began to speak to God.

'Lord, I don't know what to feel. Why am I in this place? You know Lord, you know what I went through in solitary in Sacramento. I don't think I can do this all over again. Please Lord, allow me to find a way back into the general population.' I continued to pray for my family and my children until I fell asleep.

The next morning I was woken by the door slot opening and a tray of food placed on it. It was breakfast time. I was shaking from the cold air and quickly realized that I was feeling sick. My body ached and I slowly made my way to grab the tray and sat on the stool to eat. I felt disoriented and for a moment, forgot where I was. Once the reality hit, I finished my food, put the tray back on the platform of the open slot and laid back down. Once I realized that the officer was making his rounds I waited at my door for him.

"Officer, I haven't received my issue. I don't have a toothbrush."

"We are all out, you'll have to wait for commissary to buy one."

"When is commissary?" I asked.

"Commissary sheets go out on Wednesday and you'll receive it on Friday."

"Friday!, today is Saturday," I said. I thought to myself, 'this is insane.'

"Nothing I can do about that," said the sheriff as he walked off.

Once the sheriff walked away, I heard a deep voice from the cell beside me.

"What's up man, you doing ok over there?" he asked.

I could tell from the sound of his voice that it was a black man.

"Not really. My cell is so cold, I'm getting sick, I have no hygiene products and I can't get any until Friday. What's up with this place?" I said.

"Yeah, this place is insane. You can call me Dee, I'm from Oakland. Been here for about a year now. We are in T-Sep which means total separation. As far as hygiene, I don't have any extra, but I'm sure someone will help you out... so... why did they bring you to T-Sep?"

I knew he was fishing to find out. Being brought into isolation could mean a few things. It could mean you are so violent that you can't be in the general population, it could mean you need protection from the general population, it could also mean you are a child molester or rapist, a murderer or fighting a high profile case.

In jail, there are very deeply ingrained house rules. Also rules between different races and how they communicate, and how much they communicate with each other. There is no doubt in my mind that while we were talking, others were listening also. I was the new fish, and everyone needed to know who was brought into their fish tank. I decided to answer back.

"I have no idea why I'm here. I just came from Sac county fighting a federal case for the last fifteen months. I was in the general population the entire time, besides my first forty-five days." I said this to establish that I was not in protective custody in Sacramento. "I was sentenced, but now I'm here to face the judge in San Francisco. I'm fighting a RICO case."

We continued to small talk as he also shared a little with me about his own case. He was fighting a murder charge. I never asked who, what or where. It was none of my business. After I told him about my federal case, he stopped asking questions. I shared with him that I was a Christian and I needed to get a bible. He gave me a few request forms and told me to fill them out before the officers picked up the mail. I used one of the forms to request a bible from the chaplain, the second form I wrote to the Sergeant requesting that I be put in general population. As the day progressed, I began to feel worse. By Sunday morning I had full-blown flu with fever. I was sitting in solitary with no information on how long I'd be here, when I would go to court or how much more time would be added to my sentence.

By Sunday night all I could do was lay trembling

on my bunk as I laid on a thin mattress and trying to keep warm with the thin blanket. My teeth were chattering as I was trying to sleep as I tossed and turned. This is the moment in which I first experienced the power of God first-hand through me. It would be the first of many I would experience throughout the years. I became so frustrated at my situation, the fever, the thin sheet, no pillow and the air coming out of the vent in full strength, which made the cell feel like a refrigerator. Before I could even think about how absurd it would sound, I sat up and gave a frustrated command.

"I command the air to stop in the name of Jesus, now!" the moment the words left my mouth, the air that had not stopped blowing full strength since the moment I stepped into the cell instantly went from a ten to a two. I realize that many reading this won't believe it or will find a 'rational' reason for this happening. I was in the cell, it truly happened, and I began to thank God the very moment it happened. The vent stayed that way for the rest of my time there.

Later that day I was taken out of my cell and put into a nearby holding cell. I was confused as to what was happening. A few minutes later two sheriffs walked in with my request form in his hand.

"Mr. Rocha, I came to see you about the request

form. I see that you want to be in general population. Why would you request that?" asked the Sergeant.

"I came here from Sac County, and during my time there I was in solitary for my first forty-five days. After that, I was allowed into the general population my entire time, and I was a trustee worker in my pod. I've been sentenced, brought here to face the judge in San Francisco and for some reason your officers put me here in T-Sep. I don't want to be here, and there is no reason why I should be here. I'm not a troublemaker, nor have I been written up during my fifteen months in Sacramento."

"Mr. Rocha, we know exactly who you are and we are very aware of your case. Each of your co-defendants in the RICO case cannot be allowed to be in the general population, we can't have a gang uprising here in our jail. You seem like a level headed guy, but unfortunate for you, we will not be allowing you to be in general population. All you can hope for is that your judge sees you and the marshals quickly take you to federal prison. I am not going to deal with the potential violence that could happen with such a high profile inmate like yourself... do you have any questions about my decision?" Asked the Sergeant.

I nodded my head, "No, I don't have any questions."

With the conversation now over, the officers walked out and after a few minutes, the pod officer came to take me back to my cell. The reality of it all finally became a reality. I knew that the wheels of the federal courts move slowly. I would most likely be sitting in this T-Sep for months.

Monday morning came quickly as I was awakened by an officer at my door.

"Rocha, get dressed, you got court today. You got five minutes."

I quickly woke up and brushed my teeth with my finger and no toothpaste. I washed my face and put my shoes on. When the officer came back he opened the door slot and instructed me to put my hands out of the slot so he could cuff me. Once my wrists were cuffed he opened the door and put cuffs on my ankles with a waist chain that was attached to my wrists. He proceeded to take me to the same holding cell I was in with the Sergeant the day before. It was hard to walk with not much length of chain between my ankles. I felt like a walking penguin. There was a television in the corner and a single chair in the middle of the cell.

"Marshals will be here in about thirty minutes to come to get you. Make yourself comfortable," said the officer. Then closed and locked the door behind me. I sat down and looked down at all of the chains on me. Sitting in this cell behind so many doors and corridors. I couldn't hold it anymore and began to weep.

"I can't do this Lord. Please take this from me. I don't know how to do this... I can't bear it!" The utter despair of being in solitary once again. Knowing that it would possibly be months felt like too much for my mind. I missed my children, my family, and freedom. The Lord had blessed me in Sacramento County jail with the trustee job. I was giving Bible studies to anyone that asked. My cell was never locked. The very laws were changed on the day I was to be sentenced. Yet, how could God forget me and allow me to be in this situation?

"Lord, give me strength. Be with me Jesus," I whispered as I sat with my head down. After a few minutes, I looked up and saw the television. It was built into the wall with a solid metal box around it and a thick glass in front of it, to help prevent the screen from being broken. There was a small opening that allowed the channel to be changed and the volume adjusted. I stood up and walked over. It took some stretching and positioning to be able to reach the buttons. Once turned on, I flipped the channel and stopped when I saw a preacher giving a sermon. I couldn't believe it! It was five o'clock in the morning on a Monday, and there was a pastor preaching. I sat down and began to listen.

The pastor looked directly into the camera, "I want to talk to you about Joseph. He was sold by his own brothers into slavery. His brothers hated him and threw him into a deep pit. He didn't understand at the moment, but in time he would.' Then he pointed right at the camera. The world froze for me as I intently looked on. He continued. 'You! my friend. Might find yourself in a deep dark pit right now. I have something to tell you. Even though Joseph was thrown into the deepest and darkest place he had ever known, God was about to pull him out and make him second in command under Pharoah, the king of Egypt in the future. So if that is you, if you are in a dark pit in your life right now. don't look at what you are going through, look where you are going to!'

The last line hit me like lightning. I know knew that it was God's will that I be in this holding cell, at this specific time to be encouraged. I was filled with new hope and all despair left me. I began to praise God right in that chair.

"Thank you, Jesus, Thank you, Lord. Thank you for giving me this message right now. I knew it was You talking through this pastor for me. I receive it.

Like Joseph, I am in a dark pit, but I will keep my eyes on You. I will go forward in You. Thank you, Jesus!"

What happened next will never be forgotten in my mind. As I was sitting there, in chains praising God with my eyes closed. In the spirit, I felt something pouring over me and for the first time, I began to speak in a language I had never used before. I was trying to say, 'Thank you, Jesus, praise God, I worship You.' Yet a foreign language came out of my mouth instead. I couldn't stop. I began to feel different. A new breath of life. A new strength coursing through my veins. For a moment, I forgot I was in this place. After a few minutes, I opened my eyes and realized that I was in the holding cell. I quickly looked toward the door to make sure an officer didn't see what just happened and think I was losing my mind. I gathered myself and within a few minutes, two marshals came to transport me.

I was put in a van with other inmates and we made the drive to the San Francisco Federal court building. 'What just happened?' I thought to myself. 'Was this the baptism of the Holy Spirit? Did I just speak in tongues?' I was raised in the church and had heard tongues many times in my life. I just never thought it would happen to me.

Once I was in the Federal courthouse, I was visited by my lawyer from my original RICO case.

We talked and he was able to inform me of what was going to happen, and for me to trust him. It would take a few months but he thought he could work a plea agreement and not add too much time to my ninety-month sentence. Once taken in the courtroom, I was able to quickly see my family sitting down. Once court was over, I was taken back to a holding cell, and after a few hours, we were all taken back to Santa Rita. I was put in another holding cell, given dinner then taken back into my pod.

This was the moment of truth for me. All-day long I couldn't stop thinking about my experience while listening to the preacher on the television. I sat down on my bunk, feeling better for the first time since arriving in Santa Rita.

"Lord, If what happened earlier is what I think happened. In your name let it happen again." The moment the prayer went out, it instantly happened again. I began to speak in a language that I had never learned. I often tell people this story of my baptism in the Holy Spirit. I didn't need a big revival or a worship team playing loudly. I didn't need anyone to 'coach' me into speaking in tongues. It was just Jesus and me. The Lord knew that for the next few months, without His Spirit empowering me, I would have lost my mind.

8

LEARN TO PROGRAM OR GO CRAZY

There are some basic, yet fundamental guides to staying sane while in solitary confinement. I can say it with one word, 'program'. I do not know anyone that has stayed sane while in solitary confinement without this one word. To program is to find a program within yourself for a monthly, weekly, daily hour to hour tasks that you do to fill up your day. Without doing this, you will lose track of time, days and eventually slip out of reality. This is the first thing I had to learn while in the hole. By the first month in the cell, my program was a well-oiled machine. In the morning, I would be awakened by the breakfast cart. My slot would be opened and my breakfast tray was placed there. I would wake up and sit and eat. Once I was done, I would put the tray back on the slot and lay back down for two more hours of sleep. Once I would wake up for the day, I would wash up and pray. After prayer, I would read my bible for an hour or so. By this time it was lunch and a sack was brought to the slot. I would take my time and lay it out on the table in order to take more time out of the day. I would eat it as if I was sitting in a food court. After lunch, I would sit up on my bunk and read from whatever book I had. Sometimes a novel, other times an educational or history book. Usually, a novel, which was my time for entertainment since I had no access to movies or television. The novel would allow me to escape my reality and through the story, I'd go into different parts of the world and even different eras. If dinner was still a few hours away, I would go back to read my bible and talk to God about what I was reading. Once dinner came, my entire protocol was the same as lunch. Since everyone's slot was open during dinner, it allowed many of the inmates in the pod to talk, so that was always a good time to socialize. After dinner, I would take a short nap as I digested my dinner, plus it helped to keep the day moving. After my nap, I would sit on my stool and wait for the mail to arrive. I also would write letters each day during this time. Also read any letters that I received that day, which in turn, gave me more to do in answering the letters to allow the day to pass. Once I was finished answering letters, I would tidy up my cell, clean my sink or whatever needed cleaning. After cleaning I would do some kind of light exercise on the days I wouldn't come out of my cell for a shower. (We were each supposed to have an hour each day outside of our cell to use the phone, watch television, shower or just walk around within the pod. This is why many will say, 23 and 1. Meaning you are locked down for twenty-three hours and out of your cell for one hour. It never happened. Usually, by the time my hour to get out of my cell came around, two or three days had already passed. This was because there was a rotation beginning with cell number one. He would get his hour, then the next cell and so forth. Yet with breakfast, lunch, dinner, mail, nurse visits and other reasons, it would take two or three days for the officers to actually have the time to allow everyone in the pod their individual hour. In solitary, you were never allowed to be out for your hour with anyone else.) So, in continuing with my explanation of my program, let's get back to it. I would usually get hungry later in the evening because dinner was served early, which was usually between 5 pm and 5:30 pm. So I always made sure

119

to have my noodles, chips or whatever else I needed to make a spread. Again, it was one more task to allow time to pass so I could be one day closer to finishing my sentence. I understand that reading this might seem a bit tedious. Which is exactly my point, I am trying to help those that have never been alone in a locked room to comprehend how every task, every second of your program is solely to use up time. Every second I can preoccupy my mind is one second closer to freedom. I imagine this applies to lifers also, most believing that old age then death is in sense freedom from the cell.

Once I reached my fifth month in the hole I had already witnessed a handful of men lose their minds. They would scream all night long, or bang and kick their door for hours. I remember seeing a young eighteen year old come in with a huge chip on his shoulder. He talked tough to the officers and other inmates. Whoever was out for their hour, he would call them over to his cell, if they refused he would use that persons entire hour to provoke them to argue. One day he simply snapped and became withdrawn. He wouldn't shower and refused to even come out for his hour. He would kick his door over and over. He became an empty shell of himself. I never ridiculed the guy, because I understood how easy it could happen. He simply failed to program.

It was during my sixth month, during prayer that I felt the call from God.

'David, you will preach my gospel to the world.'

It wasn't an audible voice, yet it was as real as a conversation over coffee. I didn't know how to answer.

"Lord, I don't want to preach. I don't want to be in any limelight!"

'David, I didn't ask you, I am telling you. I called you for such a time as this. I allowed you to live the life you wanted to live, and now I will use your past to pave the way for your future. I told your tia Benny that through you, many will know my power. She told you this back in Sacramento. This is how many will know that I am still the Lord. I will use you to reach many.'

I didn't want this calling. I began to disagree with God and give Him excuses as to why it shouldn't be me.

"Lord, I love you. I have been in the limelight and stage for all of my adult life. I don't want this. I want to serve you, find a place of worship, serve your people and live a peaceful life."

The Lord stopped the conversation and I figured that He understood and would leave me alone about preaching. The funny thing about God, He is very patient. A few days later I was reading in the book of Jeremiah chapter twenty and came across verse nine.

Then I said, I will not make mention of him, nor speak any more in his name. But his word was in mine heart as a burning fire shut up in my bones, and I was weary with forbearing, and I could not stay.

Jeremiah was a persecuted and hated prophet that had reached the end of his rope. He made this statement because he was sick and tired of preaching and being hated for it. Yet, within the same verse, he explains that even though he didn't want to prophesy or preach, the Word of God was like a burning fire in his bones and he couldn't hold it any longer. This verse repeated itself in my heart for the next few days. It was getting stronger and stronger to the point that I couldn't take it.

"Ok, Lord! I will preach. I will do it! But I am in solitary, who am I going to preach to?" I waited for Him to answer and I heard nothing. Yet the urge to preach was building up in my heart and soul. I began to feel like a caged lion going back and forth in my cell. I couldn't sleep or read my novel. It was hard to write letters. I didn't know what to do, so I grabbed a pencil and began writing a sermon on paper. Five or six pages later the sermon was done. This was my only avenue to preach, on paper. I began writing sermons every day and mailing them to my parents.

This became a part of my learning on how to preach. I didn't have a bible college or even a pastor to show me or instruct me. I didn't even have a study bible. I would read my Bible and ask the Lord to show me and teach me. I realized that even though I was serving the Lord the entire fifteen months in Sacramento County jail, I didn't take the time to learn the deep things of God for myself. I was so busy in giving others bible studies, and ministering to others that I never took the time to allow my roots to grow deep in Christ and in His Word. In the beginning, I despised the fact that I was put in solitary, yet the Lord allowed me to realize that I was here for a reason. If allowed to be around others, I would have continued to pour into others, yet how can I pour into others if I myself was shallow. In reading the Bible I learned that the Apostle Paul went away in the desert for three years before he began his ministry. Even for worship, I didn't know any Christian worship or praise songs. Instead, I would make lyrics up and sing them in my cell to God. He became my best friend, comforter, counselor and teacher.

Inside of my heart and mind, I felt liberated and powerful, yet treated like a beast in the reality of the jail. Each week my parents and children would visit. No matter if anyone from the pod was going to a visit, court, nurse or down the hall. We were treated like wild animals, no matter what our crimes were. The very fact that we were in T-Sep, the most controlled high-security unit in the entire jail meant that officers had to be on high alert any time one of us was taken out of our cell. There was protocol on how to open our cell and cuff us for transport. First, there were always two officers. Before they opened your door you are told to put your hands out of the slot. Cuffs were put on your wrists. Then you were told to walk to the end of your cell and face the wall as they opened the cell door. The officers would step into the cell and put cuffs on your ankles. Then once you were secured, they would take you to wherever you needed to go. During visits, my family would be sitting down with a thick glass between us. They would see the officers bring me in with cuffs on. Once again I was told to stand in the visiting booth, wait for the door to close behind me, put my hands through the slot and the cuffs were taken off of me. The visits were for thirty minutes. Living like this became normal, as the reality of life outside in the free world was blurring.

There is one thing that happens while incarcerated, especially in solitary confinement. You are left to deal with yourself. There are no outside distractions. No music, parties, social life, vacations or traveling. There is absolutely nothing. So most don't realize that when dealing with themselves, this means really looking at yourself for the first time. It's exactly why we fill our days with distractions. Because deep down, we really do not want to face the reality of who we are. It forces one to think back on what leads you to the current situation you are in. Moments are replayed in your mind as you lay on your bunk. Memories pass through your mind like shooting stars. You try to pause it, yet as soon as you see it, it fades away.

I thought back to 1989, the year my first daughter was born. I had dropped out of high school and was about to become a new father. By this time gang life in Tracy was the norm. At one point, the small town of Tracy was completely united amongst the Chicanos. This didn't last very long once my generation began growing up. My perspective of the OG (original gangster) was one of awe. My brothers were cholos, their friends were cholos and that's what I was going to be. It was so twisted because it was every young cholos dream to be a part of the big prison gangs from my area. They would come out after being away for years and be respected and feared. If there was a house party and one of them would walk in, the mood would change and everyone made sure to pay respect and shake their hand. This was the influence that paved the way I would live my life. I learned things about how to handle myself and demeanor. To never show fear no matter what. I stayed sober so I could always be alert to my surroundings. To never put your back to the door in a public place in case an enemy walked in.

With a new baby girl to care for, I figured I'd do the responsible thing and get a job. Two years had passed and I was now twenty years old. My rap career hadn't yet begun. Things were going well until one day my supervisor informed me that it was the last day for the company. He handed me my final check and sent me home. I was frustrated. I was a new father, newly married with responsibilities of rent and a car payment. What was I going to do now? I searched for work and became more frustrated and angry as the days passed with no employment. This was the time I decided to take my fate into my own hands. I went to visit a friend and he schooled me on selling weed. I am a quick learner, so before I knew it I had surpassed him in sales with a better connection supplying me. I always describe these years as the rollercoaster years. When you first get on a ride, it begins slow and makes it's way up the first hill. You can hear the clicking as the coaster goes higher and higher. Then there is a moment of pause at the very top. Before you know it, the coaster goes straight down with twists and turns as it gains momentum. This is how I always describe my life. A ride that continued to gain momentum, with twists and turns with no end in sight. I was a gangster, weed dealer and beginning to gain recognition for my music as I began to perform at local lowrider car shows throughout northern California. It was a perfect storm that was about to bring damage to so many people. I had a dream and goal of being the most known Chicano rapper in the world. I would make music for my people. I felt that the rap culture left Chicanos on the outskirts, yet we were all buying and listening to artists that had nothing to do with our Raza.

After a few months of performing in places like Stockton, Manteca, Modesto, San Jose, and Sacramento, the crowds that would gather was growing. I began to feel as if I really had a future in the music industry. I would simply write about what I was feeling and seeing in my day to day life. Lyrics came to me easily.

One day my phone rang and it was my Tia Benny, sister to my father. She was like a mother to me. A Christian believer and was the most powerful prayer warrior I would ever know. She would lock herself in her room in prayer for days at a time while fasting. She lived in section-8 government housing and worked at a cannery, yet a powerhouse for the Kingdom of God.

I heard weeping over the phone when I answered. I couldn't figure out what was going on. She was trying to speak but her crying made it nearly impossible to hear what she was trying to say to me. I realized it was her and instantly panicked. I thought something had happened to her or to my cousins.

"Tia! Tia! Is everything okay? Is Nick ok? Did something happen to him?" I yelled into the phone.

She began to calm down enough to be understandable and said, "I saw you die mijo! I saw you die!"

"I'm okay, I'm here at home. I'm okay!" I said.

"She began speaking again between sobs. "You don't understand. God showed me a vision. I have been fasting and in prayer in my room. I saw you rise to the top with the help of satan. You wouldn't listen to me and continued to go up a high mountain... then... then... at the very top, you thought you were safe and the devil threw you off of the top and you fell. You fell! I saw you die!" She began weeping again in anguish.

"That doesn't make any sense tia. I'm okay and I'm here at home." This startled me. She had no idea about my plans to rise in the music industry. She lived forty-five minutes away and had no idea I had begun performing in local car shows. I always believed in God and I never doubted Jesus existed. I felt my heart beating rapidly in my chest. I knew this was a prophetic word. Having grown up in a Christian home, I knew without a shadow of a doubt that this was real.

She continued. "David, I don't know what you are doing or what you are involved in. Please promise me that you will go to your room and pray. Ask God to reveal this vision to you. Promise me that you won't follow satan no matter what he offers you."

I wanted to calm her down, so I said, "Okay tia, I promise. Please don't worry about me. I'm okay."

"Okay mijo, I love you so much," And she hung up the phone. I walked into my room and sat on my bed. I began to speak to God. I soon felt tears falling down my eyes.

"Jesus, why are you doing this to me? This isn't fair. My music career is just beginning, people are listening to me. This is the only thing I want in this world and You want to take it away from me. Jesus, I believe in you. I know that you are God... but I need to follow through on this path. I will be careful, and I want you to be with me. Either way, I'm going to follow through. Maybe if I live to follow you when I'm old then I'll do it. For now, I need to follow my heart so I can make enough money to live a good life for myself and my family. I'm sorry Jesus." I sat at the edge of my bed for a few minutes. I knew deep down inside that following a rap career was going to be the end of me. If this was inevitable, so be it. I would run toward my early death head-on for the world to see and leave a legacy like no other.

Within a few months of that phone call and the talk with God, fame came very quickly. I was twenty-one years old and meeting with some local rappers. We came up with an amazing plan. I had a local following in the Tracy area, one of the other rappers had a local following in the San Francisco area, a handful of the others had a local following in the East Bay area. We figured that if we would make a group album, share each other's followers, it would instantly combine our fans and we could lock down our corner of the market. In all actuality, I was ready to quit my rap career before it had begun. One day I heard a knock on my door and it was two rappers I knew from performing at car shows. They convinced me to pursue music and within weeks we were off and running. I began headlining concerts, switched from selling weed to selling methamphetamine. On the street, it was known as crank, and those addicted to it couldn't get enough of it. By 1993, I and a group of local rappers from the valley and Bay Area owned our own studio and signed a nationwide deal for our project, From the Barrio with Love. This caused our group Darkroom Familia to catapult to be a supergroup with sales across the country. The rollercoaster was in hyperspeed mode by this time. I was losing myself and becoming Sir Dyno. I began flying to perform in concerts, autograph signing events at records stores, and writing lyrics that caused a shockwave across Chicano barrios everywhere.

My life became a twisted race for power and respect. It didn't take long to realize the influence my music and lyrics had over my peers. Our label had nationwide distribution for our music and we began producing movies with major distribution also. I was rising in fame and in the drug game. Before I knew it, I was buying meth from a direct connection from Mexico and flying across the country for concerts, autograph signing, and business. The most troubling was that the music industry in northern California was so intertwined with criminals, drug dealers and prison gangs, that it was a fine line of saying the wrong thing on a song, or being around the wrong person that was deemed no good within the prison system or neighborhood. Murders were a common thing within the structured web that hovered over northern California, many times committed by those closest to the victim. My entire life and career were under this cloud of darkness that permeated the very fabric of our culture. The music I produced had an entire generation in a trance, with my CD at many taped off crime scenes. My generation used the music we released as a soundtrack to violence across many southwestern states. Parents and teachers protested in front of music stores against our releases. This simply ignited more interest and more fans to follow. None of these facts are bragging rights. In reality, it weighs heavily on me. To know that many are dead or in prison because of the influence of my lyrics is not an easy pill for me to swallow. If I could turn back time for so many broken families, I would.

I saw my entire life as a movie as I laid on my bunk in my cell. By month eight, I myself began to lose my sense of reality. A homeless man was put in the cell next to me that talked to himself constantly. What was odd was that he would have conversations with himself and it sounded as if three people lived in his solitary cell. I would always pray because I knew that this man was possessed by demons. All-day and night I could hear his voices arguing amongst themselves. One day I woke up to do my program and I couldn't stay on track. I felt myself becoming numb to my situation. I would sit on my bunk and stare at the walls for hours before snapping myself out of it. The days began to blend into each other. I would open my bible to read and none of it made sense. I would try to write letters and would stare at the paper and pencil in front of me with no words to write. I would try to pray and it felt as if I couldn't concentrate. I didn't know what was going on with me. During visits, my family looked worried. I had not had a haircut for almost a year so my hair reached down to my nose if I combed it over my face. Usually, I was excited to get a visit, but now I had no words to share and I continually looked down as I held the phone to my ear to talk with them through the glass. It felt like a dark fog was in my head, not allowing me to think right. At night I'd lay on the bottom bunk and kick the empty bunk above me over and over just to hear the noise. Sometimes I would stand at my door and kick it repeatedly for no reason at all. Things began to happen in my cell that couldn't be explained in the natural world. Once I was trying to pray on my bunk and my pencil flew off of my desk and across the cell. The man next to me was getting louder each day with his multiple voices.

The episode came to a climax after a visit from my children and their mother. I had just come back from the visit, was in my cell for a short while and then it so happened that it was my turn to be out in the pod for my hour. My door popped open and I grabbed my towel to shower. The moment I finished my shower, I walked straight to the phone. I felt agitated because, in my mind, nobody had visited me for over two weeks. I called my house and my children's mother picked up the phone. She sounded cheerful. Before I gave her a chance to speak I started in.

"Why haven't you visited! It's been two weeks since you've been here, my parents haven't visited. What's going on with everyone!" I said aggressively into the phone.

"What are you talking about? I was just there with the kids a couple of hours ago. Are you being serious right now? What's wrong with you!"

My mind began reeling, what was she talking about? Is she playing mind games with me? Does she think this is a joke?

"I don't know what you are talking about. All I know is that I'm sitting in this cell and nobody has come to see me. Don't you realize that a visit allows me to come out of my cell? I'm going to go crazy in here!" I said.

She began to cry. "I'm going to call your mom. You are scaring me!"

"I don't need you to call my mom! I just need you to visit! I gotta go now. Hope you find the time to visit."

I hung up the phone and began pacing in the pod.

My neighbor to my left, the black man from Oakland called me over to his door. I walked over.

"David, What's going on man? I've never seen you like this. I know I don't serve God like you, but I believe in God and I respect that you are a Christian."

"Bro, you know how it is in here sitting in this cell all day. I don't know what my family is thinking about not visiting," I answered.

My neighbor looked confused. "You just had a visit like two hours ago... David, are you okay?"

"What do you mean. It's been two weeks since I've had a visit," I answered.

"Listen, David. I'm not one to play games with you or anyone else. You just left on a visit about two hours ago. I don't know if you need sleep or what, but you had a visit two hours ago."

My pod time was now over and I locked myself back into my cell. None of this made sense. I tried to pray and felt too clouded in my mind to pray. Within two hours I was surprised to be called to a visit from my parents. They were concerned and made their way before visiting was over for the day. The visit was a blur as my parents prayed over me through the phone and glass as they wept. I didn't feel a thing, I was numb. Once the visit was over I went back to my cell and fell asleep.

The next day began with my neighbor loudly talking to himself again. Once the evening came, I was called for another visit. I had no idea who was visiting, but I realized I was wrong the day before. I did have a visit, yet I couldn't understand how I couldn't remember. Once I was led up the stairs to the visiting book I saw my children and my mom. Once the cuffs were taken off I sat down, put the phone receiver to my ear and held my head down. I didn't want my kids to see me like this.

She began to speak, "David, talk to me."

"I don't feel like talking. This is too much. Everything is too much," I answered reluctantly.

"David! Look at me... now!" she said with anger and authority.

I slowly looked up at her and the kids. The kids were smiling and waving at me.

She began to speak. "I don't know what you are feeling, I don't know what it is like for you in there. But what I do know is that you are not a quitter. You are stronger than this place! You are a strong man. You are loved and you are a father to these beautiful children. They need you! We need you! Your older daughters need you! All of this will be over someday. We all need you... so snap out of it! Fight whatever you have to fight!"

In that instant, something changed. My children

each got on the phone receiver to talk to me. I saw happiness in their eyes to see me. I saw hope in them. I'm not an animal, I'm a man. I'm not a loser, I am a father. Even though I was locked in this jail, in the eyes of my children I was still their hero. I began to weep as the fog in my mind began to roll away. I went back to my cell and instantly opened my Bible. I was able to read it. I sat on my bunk and prayed, which made sense to me once again.

"Thank you, Jesus. You have delivered me and set me free once again. Lord, I don't know what came over me, but I never want that to happen again. I rebuke any spirit or demon in this entire pod in the name of Jesus. I proclaim the blood of Jesus in my cell. I declare for my cell to be holy ground. I command the demons in the cell next door to shut their mouths and leave in the name of Jesus."

A few days after this happened, the man next door was taken out of the cell and moved to a different location. I again began to grow strong in the Lord as I continued to write sermons and study my bible in prayer. The more that I learned, the more I desired to have at least one brother in Christ to fellowship with. I wasn't asking for an entire congregation, just one single brother. I know that God is faithful, so I couldn't wait for the day God would answer my prayer.

9

MY ASSASSIN LIVES NEXT DOOR

Once the man with many voices was transferred to a different location, the cell was empty for two weeks. I fell right back into my program. My older brother Ruben had sent me a book on drawing animals, I figured it was a good thing to add to my program. I used the book as a textbook and walked through every single step before going onto the next page or chapter. I found it very therapeutic. I had always wanted to learn to draw, what better time than now.

As I was drawing after dinner one day, I heard the officers coming into the pod. They had a new inmate with them. He was an older Chicano with a battle-worn presence about him. His mustache and goatee were long and had the look of a hardened prison veteran. He saw me looking out of my window and he was being taken to the cell next to me. He nodded his head and I nodded back. For the sake of this book, I am going to use the name, Mike.

We began to talk daily. We were able to hear each other clearly if we both stood at our door. He didn't have any money on his books so I ordered him some soups and coffee when commissary came around. As a favor for what I ordered for him, he began giving me lessons on drawing. He saw that I was very interested in learning so he taught me some tips. He had been in state prison over the last ten years and was back in court for a motion that he filed. In state prison, he was serving his time in a high-security prison level, which is why he was put into T-sep when he was brought to this county jail. I knew that he was an active homie, so I knew that even though he was friendly, didn't actually mean we were friends. Nevertheless, I treated him as a friend and soon enough I began to share Jesus with him. This began as a question about the Bible here and there and turned into full-blown Bible studies that would last hours at a time. This went on for a period of four weeks.

One day when he was out for his hour, which was

right before my hour, he walked up to my door after his shower.

"David, you busy?" he knocked on my door. I was on my bunk reading a book.

"No, what's going on?" I said as I walked up to the door. He had a look of concern that I had never seen on his face before. When you are next to someone for four weeks in a place like this, friendships can grow very quickly.

He looked at me hesitantly, then finally spoke. "I just want to apologize to you. I'm sorry."

I was confused. I had no idea what he was sorry about or why he felt he needed to apologize. "Sorry for what?" I asked.

He lowered his voice and began to explain it to me. "I am supposed to take you out bro. Some of the higher-ups don't like the fact that you left the cause to follow Jesus. I was given a wila (small message in small writing called micro-writing and rolled up so they can be transported from pod to pod or even prison to prison through inmates). They found out that I am in the pod with you and that I come out for my hour right before you. I'm supposed to figure out a way to rig my door to open once you are out for your hour... I'm so sorry bro."

I took a deep breath. I know how the homies function, and I had to be very wise and use discernment, knowing that a wrong word or move could end with me in a body bag.

I said, "Why are you telling me this? If this is what you are supposed to do, why tell me?"

He continued. "Because you are a good dude. I was supposed to earn your trust so that way you wouldn't suspect anything when it was time. I respect you bro and most of all... I want to surrender to Jesus as you did. I'm tired of this life. I want what you have. The things you teach me are things I've never heard before. The way you put it makes sense."

I looked at him to make sure it was real. So many thoughts came rushing into my head. What if this was part of the plan? I had to make up my mind here and now if I truly believed in the power of Jesus Christ. The Bible says in John chapter one that Jesus is the light, and darkness does not comprehend the light. Could it truly be that this man befriended me with bad intentions, yet the light was too bright for him to deny?

"Mike, if what you are saying is what is truly in your heart, you can surrender right now to Jesus. Today can be the first day of the rest of your life."

"Yes bro, yes. I want to surrender right now," he answered.

"Okay, I am going to guide you through prayer. This prayer means nothing unless you mean it with all of your heart. God hears your heart more than the words that come out of your mouth. According to the Bible, he will take out your heart of stone, take your pain, your suffering and will replace it with a heart of flesh. Then He says that He will put His Spirit within you. Do you believe this?" I asked Him.

"Yes, I believe you," he said.

"Okay, then repeat after me. Jesus, I come to you as a humble man. I surrender myself and my life to you. I know that you are real. I believe that you died on the cross for me, to wash away my sins in your blood. And after three days, I believe that you rose again to power. I repent of all my sins I have ever committed against you. I turn away from my old life. From now on I will follow you until my last breath. Live in me, Jesus. Make me the man that you created me to be. In Jesus' name, amen."

As we finished the prayer, his hour was up and he had to lock it down. I was so excited for him and for myself. To think that God found me worthy enough to lead someone to Him. All of heaven was rejoicing according to the Bible. I felt rejuvenated. Darkness wanted to destroy me, and Jesus was stronger than darkness.

He began to speak, "I feel so free now! Thank you so much, for all you've taught me. I will never forget this. I guess God had other plans for putting me next to you. If anyone wants to do something to you, they will have to get both of us."

"Amen brother Mike, Amen."

We continued to fellowship and study together. Not only did the Lord use me to save this brother, but it also caused my prayer to be answered. I wanted one brother to fellowship with, and here it happened. The Bible says that God will give you the desires of your heart. He also shared with me that he's never had a visit in years. During a visit, I shared with my parents about Mike surrendering his life to Jesus. They immediately asked for his information and mailed him a Bible. To top it off, my parents came for a visit, and my dad pulled him out at the same time my mom came to see me. Mike finally had a visit, and my dad was able to minister to him by sharing his own testimony with Mike. He was so excited when they came to get him out of the cell. Visits were only thirty minutes long, but it felt like heaven for him to actually be able to be free from the cage.

Our fellowship was short-lived after that. He was taken to his court date and sent back to prison soon after. There are no coincidences in the Kingdom of God. I knew now that there was no stopping the plan and calling that God has laid out for me. What the enemy meant to destroy me, God used it for good. Satan wanted to use this man to take me out, but God is stronger than hate. He is my protector and my shield. God protected me in Sacramento County Jail, here from someone with direct orders to do me harm, and He would continue to protect me until I fulfill in life what I am supposed to fulfill for His Kingdom.

10

CON AIR -I WILL SOAR ABOVE THE CLOUDS AND BE FREE

I was finally sentenced in the San Francisco Federal Courthouse. I pled guilty to committing a crime while on federal bond and was given eighteen months. One year would be concurrent with my ninety-month sentence, and six months would be added which brought my entire sentence to ninety-six months, or eight years. In the Federal Bureau of Prisons, there is no early parole, only probation once you have finished your sentence. Each person must do eighty-five percent of their prison sentence across the board, with one exception, the residential drug program (RDAP). My lawyer requested that I be admitted into RDAP, which is a program within the prison system that allows a twelve-month reduction, only if the inmate graduates a nine-month program. My judge agreed and recommended the program once I was taken into a federal prison that offered it. This was the big issue, even if the judge recommended the RDAP program for you, it didn't necessarily mean it was available to you. There are now thousands of inmates with a recommendation for RDAP, pouring into the prison system with a limited amount of seats for the nine-month program. The line to get in is so congested, the request to be transferred to a prison that offers it is so unlikely, that many inmates that actually get transferred to a functioning RDAP, don't get the full benefit. Due to the fact that by the time they got to the program in order to begin the nine-month classes, they had already served most of their time anyway.

I was also given some 'time served credit' from the moment I was arrested and taken to Sacramento County Jail, which put me at two years accounted for my sentence. By the time the Marshals came to pick me up, I had now been in T-sep for eleven and a half months. It felt weird to walk out of my cell. I felt confused because a part of me didn't want to leave. I had learned to like my cell like a safe cocoon. I slowly walked out and looked back before I walked off. I said my good-byes to the men that I had made friends with and walked out of Santa Rita for the last time. I once again saw the long corridor that led to the booking as the marshals put a group of us into a van. I was done with solitary confinement, done with this place and on to finish off my time in federal prison. I was actually looking forward to being free to walk in a prison yard and eat my meals in a chow hall. The big question in my mind, and in the minds of the men in the van was, where are we going to be transported to. We all knew that we could be sent to any federal prison in the fifty states. I held my breath as one of the inmates asked, "Marshal... can you tell us where we are going?"

The marshal answered quickly. "You are all going to Oakland North Jail until further notice."

Everyone in the van became quiet after that. If any place was worse than Santa Rita, it was the Oakland North Jail. I had spent thirty days in this jail before and was not looking forward to this place again. It felt as if it was designed to look and feel like a dungeon. Sitting in the center of downtown Oakland, next to freeway 880. It was a giant slab of concrete with slits for windows. The second you walked in, it felt like you were walking into a giant underground concrete laden apocalyptic insane asylum. The air in the building sucked the life out of you. We were each booked and taken to our individual cells. Once again, I was taken to solitary confinement and put into a medieval-looking dungeon made of concrete. By this time I was not bothered with solitary. It was the only life I knew. As soon as I got a chance, I called home to let my family know that I was transported to the Oakland jail. I had to leave all of my commissary back in Santa Rita, so once again I had to order hygiene and snacks with the money I had on my books. I was told that my stay here would only be a few days, possibly up to two weeks. It was nothing I couldn't handle. I simply created a new program and began to follow it so the days would pass. I had no Bible, but I was able to study and pray because I now had much of the Word of God in my heart and mind. This place couldn't break me, not because I was strong, but because I could do all things through Christ that gives me strength.

The days in Oakland moved along like clockwork. I was able to minister to a man on the left of my cell. The pods were smaller, so I was actually able to get my hour out of my cell each day. To the reader, I know an hour a day out of your cell doesn't sound like much. Yet to me, it felt like freedom. Having an hour each day to shower, use the phone and actually watch television for a few minutes felt like I was a king. I was there exactly two weeks before the sheriffs woke me up to get ready for transport. The marshals were on their way to get me.

Two years had now passed since my arrest and I no longer felt out of my element. Life incarcerated became my norm. I didn't like it, but it was what it was. I was ready to go to prison now. Sometimes in life, you don't realize how far you've gone until you actually look back. With two years of concrete, locked doors, visits through glass windows, letters and phone calls, a change has to happen. I became a different person in this place. Some for the better, some damaged me in my mind and changed my perspective of life in a way that most won't understand. To be honest, parts of me have never left that place of solitary. I don't like admitting this, and for the first time, many of my loved ones are hearing this for the first time as they read it. Solitary confinement has been declared by the United Nations to be classified as torture. Two years since I was free might seem minuscule, but it felt a lifetime away. I remember back to the first time I drove to Los Angeles. Once you pass Bakersfield you can see the Grapevine. It is a gigantic mountain range that separates northern and southern California. There is one large freeway that passes right through it, the most important artery for transportation, shipping, and travel in the state of California. As you approach the mountain, it looms high and far to the right and left. As I drove forward, I was waiting to actually begin the incline to go up. What I didn't notice until I looked back, was that I had already begun the incline many miles back. It was so gradual that I hadn't noticed how far up I was. It was the same in my life now. I have come a long way as a man, as a believer of Jesus and as a survivor of Solitary confinement and incarceration.

After a few minutes of gathering myself, I was put into a holding cell until the marshals arrived. There was a handful of us that were put into the van with shackles, waist chains, and handcuffs. The minute we were all secured, the marshal in the passenger seat read off a list of our names to make sure we were all in the vehicle. I confirmed my name when he called it out. Once all of us were confirmed, he began to go down another list. The list we were all anxiously waiting for, our destinations. Many names were called before mine and each was told a different prison, with some being out of state. My heart began to beat faster. 'Please, Lord. Let me stay in California so I can see my family. Please, Lord, send me to a place that offers RDAP'

I heard my name called, "Rocha... you'll be going to Terminal Island."

I couldn't believe it. My prayers were answered. Terminal Island was in Southern California, which meant I would still be able to see my loved ones. I knew it wouldn't be often, due to the fact that Terminal Island was near Long Beach which was a good six or seven-hour drive from Tracy. I rejoiced because at least it was driving distance. I took a deep breath and relaxed for the ride. Now my only desire was the find out if they offered RDAP. The reason we were not told of our individual destinations before we were secured in the van was for safety reasons. One could plot an escape with outside help. This is why each time we were transported by marshals, the passenger held a semi-automatic tactical weapon as we drove through the streets.

Oakland wasn't a far drive to Travis Air Force base right outside of Fairfield California. Once we arrived, I noticed other buses and vans filled with inmates. Marshals surrounded the passenger plane holding shotguns as we lined up outside. Even though it looked like a regular plane you would see at any airport, this one had a special name, Con-air.

We were asked our name, inmate numbers, as they checked on a list. Then we were told to walk up the stairs to board the plane. Flying around the country was a normal thing I enjoyed, never did I think I would be in a flying prison. I was blessed to get a window seat. One thing I hated was when marshals transport you from jail to jail, to court or here on Con-air. They always put your cuffs in the black box. This allowed no movement for your wrists because it wrapped around the chain between the cuffs and forced your wrists to clamp together. I lost feeling in my thumbs before the plane lifted off. I tried to ignore it the moment I was able to look down at the beautiful view of California from up above. As I looked out I thought of the creativeness of God. The shapes and colors of rivers, mountains, and flatland. I looked out toward the horizon and saw complete blue with no cloud in sight. We were told not to talk, which allowed me to completely forget I was in shackles and chains. I forgot I was on my way to prison. I was soaring and free. I was above and not below. I felt inspired with a feeling that everything was going to be alright. God did pave a way for me and He was with me. I thought of my children and my family. Of my future, which I was grateful for. Many on this plane would never be released. Someday I would sit at a window seat just like this, but my destination would be to share Jesus to the world.

We landed in Victorville Ca, which is in southern

California. There was a line of buses and vans ready to transport everyone on the plane to different destinations. I was put into a bus and taken to another county jail that housed federal inmates, San Bernandino.

San Bernardino was like nothing I had ever seen. It was one giant cell with hundreds of inmates walking around. The bunks were stacked three high and I was given a middle bunk. The bunk above me was literally about five inches from my face. I tried to sleep and the noise of deafening. It was a complete contrast from solitary. The toilets and showers were out in the open and filthy. I had no idea how much time I would spend at that place, but I knew I had to learn to adapt. After tossing and turning on my bunk I was awaked with sheriffs coming in to count before taking us to breakfast. Soon we were marched in a single file line to the chow hall that was full of inmates from other giant cells already eating. We were told to not talk, not share food and not look up from your plate. You were given a set amount of time to eat and taken back to the open pod. Once I got back to settle in, my name was called out as well as others. Our transport bus had arrived to take us to Terminal Island federal prison. Goodbye San Bernandino, I hope I never see you again.

11

TERMINAL ISLAND, I AM HERE IN BODY BUT FREE IN THE SPIRIT

As the bus pulled into Terminal island, located between Long Beach and San Pedro I finally was able to get a good look at the outside, before we were taken in. The huge complex sat in a long rectangle shape with water surrounding it on all sides except the entrance, which was a small road in the midst of the miles and miles of shipping docks for importing and exporting. It was painted in a yellowish off white with two very high fences and multiple rows upon rows of barbed wire. The prison had been built in 1938 for federal inmates, but during WWII it was used by the United States navy for court-martialed inmates. Then in 1950, it was turned over to the state of California as a medical and psychiatric institution. Then finally in 1955, it was turned back over to the Federal Bureau of Prisons to be a low and medium-security correctional center. Terminal Island has housed known mobsters such as Al Capone, members of the Bonanno and Gambino mafia families and many other 'made' guys. It was also home to Charles Manson for two years, before the famous murders that he orchestrated. There was a lot of history in these walls, and you could feel it.

We were told to step out of the bus in line as guards stood around us holding shotguns. We were marched in and taken into a holding tank for processing. We were each taken out of our cells and given a rundown of the prison and how things work. My name was called and I walked over to the door. I was taken into a room and told to sit down.

The man was dressed sharply in his uniform, I would later find out he was a high ranking Correctional officer.

"Why are you in my prison!" asked the man.

The question confused me. I sure didn't come to 'his' prison because I wanted to be here. I stayed quiet figuring if I said anything, it would be taken as sarcasm.

"I'm sitting here going through your record, and I don't understand why you are here. I should ship you out of here today, to higher-level security. I know where you come from and I know what you guys are about!" he said.

I felt nervous. The thought of being put into isolation again for the rest of my sentence was unbearable. "Sir, I am here just to do my time. Look at my record, I have no violent felonies, I have no disciplinary actions toward me. I have been a model inmate with no issues at all for the last two years. I want to be here in California, I want to be able to see my family. I haven't hugged my children in two years."

He thought long and hard. "If I even think you are going to be an issue, I will send you to the other side of the country. We just had a riot a few months ago and I sent busloads out of here. Do not make me regret anything... go back to the holding cell."

I breathed deeply, not realizing I had been holding my breath the entire time.

"Thank you, I appreciate it," I said as I was taken back.

After everyone was processed, we were told to follow the guard so we could be given our clothes, shoes, and a blanket. As we entered into the prison, it was the first time I was out in the open air with no cuffs or ankle cuffs. I looked around and saw inmates in khaki color pants and shirts minding their business. I could smell the ocean with every breath. All I could think about was how good God has been to me. I had built such an intimate relationship with Jesus that I would say things to Him like, 'Lord, we made it out of solitary.' I would use the word 'we' when speaking about the things I would experience. No matter how often family and friends wrote letters or visited, of which I was so appreciative. I knew that the only one that served every second, every moment was Christ. We had come this far together.

Once we received our issue of clothes, boots, pillow, and blanket we were each given a unit to report to. There would be no cells in this place. Dorm living. The prison is separated into Units, each unit is divided into unit one and unit two. I was told to go into the unit that was upstairs from the laundry department. As I walked up the stairs I could hear that the unit was full of activity. My hair while in solitary was the longest it had ever been my entire life. I knew that I needed a haircut immediately. I also knew that I was deep in southern California. While I was in the world, these people were my enemies. I had to be careful. I walked over to my bunk and opened my empty locker. The freedom of just being around other humans felt strange. A Chicano came by to greet me.

"How you doing bro?" he asked.

"Doing good, just need a haircut," I answered.

"Yeah, there's a few barbers here. Where are you from?" he quickly asked. This is the first question you will be asked in any jail or prison. They want to know right away if you are an enemy or a friend.

I answered. "I'm from Christ."

"What do you mean? Are you a homie?" he said.

"I'm a believer in Jesus. Been serving the Lord for two years now," I answered.

He looked a bit frustrated and walked away. I continued to fix my bed. I sensed someone behind me so I turned around. It was an older Chicano with a long goatee and big mustache. He began to talk very calmly, collected and respectful.

"How you doing bro?" he asked in the exact same words as the guy that came up before him.

I reached out and shook his hand. I said, "I'm good. Been in a cell for the past two years, and solitary for the past year. So not really sure how to feel. I need a haircut and need to figure out who is who and what is what in this place."

"That's all good homie, but you were asked where you are from. My homie said that you said, Christ. I respect that, but we need to know who is who when someone walks into here," he said.

I nodded and answered. "I'm a believer of Jesus but I come from Tracy, up north."

He stroked his goatee while trying to figure me out. I showed no body language that would be taken as a threat, nor one of fear. I was just happy to be out of a cell, happy to be talking with someone face to face, happy with the fact that I was out of jail and in a prison with a yard, chapel, library, weight pile, and no cells.

"He said, "Okay, I have someone that can hook you up with a haircut. There are some homies from up north you might want to talk to, they hang out in the south yard. There's also a lot of Christian brothers here also."

"Thank you brother, I appreciate the info and the haircut," I answered.

He asked me to follow him to the other side of the unit and asked one of the homies to cut my hair. Usually, in prison a barber will charge stamps or items from the commissary list, this haircut would be as a favor. He let the homie know that I just got in from solitary. He might have paid him without me knowing. After the haircut, I thanked him and made my way to the shower. While brushing my teeth I saw a younger man than myself walk into the bathroom.

He washed his hands, and without looking at me, said. "Do you believe in Jesus Christ?"

"Yes, I surrendered my life to Jesus on Feb 25th, 2004," I said.

He dried his hands, looked at me and held out his hand. "Then that means that you are my brother... My name is Jacobo."

He also lived in the same unit and was watching me when I was approached by the southsiders. He explained how the prison worked. Each day for breakfast, you can come out of the unit to the chow hall, eat and go anywhere within the prison. A job would be assigned to you, depending on the job it would be for as little as an hour, or a full eight hours. There was a chapel, a library, yard with basketball courts, running track, weight pile and cardio machines. There was another section with handball courts and bleachers. There was also an in-house dentist and hospital staffed with doctors and nurses for appointments. Once at each hour was what they called a 'five-minute movement.' This meant that wherever you went, once movement was over, you had to stay there until the next hour. If you want to stay in your unit, you can. Then if you feel like going to the yard, you have to wait until movement. Once you hear the bell, you have five minutes to get to the yard. Once movement is over, you are stuck in the yard until the next hour. Besides locking down into our unit for one hour before dinner, We were able to be out of our units between 6 am and 9 pm. That is a whole lot of freedom for someone that's been in a cell for two years.

He also explained that there was a group of brothers that he fellowshipped with every day. They would be excited to meet me after dinner. They would meet at 6 pm by a group of picnic tables, next to the basketball courts and fellowship, sing worship songs and preach. I couldn't believe it. I wasn't sure if I was going to meet one brother in Christ, and now Jacobo was telling me that they had a group of believers.

"Do you want me to show you around the prison yard? It's about to be movement, we can go right now," said Jacobo.

"Yeah, let's go," I answered.

We headed toward the door as the CO (correctional officer) opened the door for anyone leaving the unit. I followed Jacobo as we walked next to other units and buildings. When we reached the south yard we all had to go through a metal detector. The last thing the prison officials wanted was for any metal prison shanks to be brought into the yard, the place most riots happen at.

From the yard, I could see the ocean and cargo boats coming and going. The entire yard was surrounded by fences and coils of barb wire. A few hundred inmates were walking, running, playing basketball and just standing in groups talking amongst themselves. Jacobo took me on a tour showing me around the entire place. I saw a group of about eight guys standing around joking and talking and instantly knew they were from northern California. I don't know how I knew, but I did. I asked Jacobo if he could give me a few minutes to talk to the group. He looked hesitant, but nodded his head and walked off to talk to someone he recognized. I took a deep breath and walked toward the group. As I approached closer they recognized that I was coming closer to them. They stopped talking and acknowledged me with head nods.

"Hey guys, I just figured that you all are from up north," I asked.

"One of them nodded, "I'm from Stockton." He had light skin with tattoos covering his arms, neck, and parts of his face.

"I'm David Rocha, from Tracy," I said. "Many people know me as Dyno."

Their demeanor changed and they all smiled. Some stuck out their hands to shake mine.

"What's up homie," said one of them. He had a serious face, solid shoulders, and eyes of a hawk.

I hesitated and thought out my words before I spoke. Everything that was about to happen would depend on how well I verbalized myself in the next few seconds.

"Well, I just came to talk to you all because I want to share something. I'm sure you know about my case. I've been sitting in Sac County and Santa Rita for the past two years. I kept my mouth shut and sat in an active pod the entire time, but in Rita, I was placed in the hole because of the high profile case. I have a ninety-six-month sentence. I surrendered my life to Jesus Christ and that's how I'm going to live my life from this moment on. I just wanted you to hear it from me. I just got here a few hours ago and I don't want another hour to pass without talking to you all. I wouldn't want you to think I had something to hide. I am here. I just want to do my time, but if me following Jesus is going to be a problem, then we might as well get it over with now. I completely understand the repercussions of my choices."

I had no idea what was going to happen next. What I did had nothing to do with bravery, it was everything to do with survival. I calculated that I would get a better response by approaching them like a man, rather than hiding in the shadows my entire time until someone recognized me, which would then make it look like I was avoiding, or worse hiding from them.

I braced myself but nothing happened. The shot-caller of the group now spoke up.

"Do you know what you are saying?" he asked as he stepped closer. "There are over two hundred southsiders on this yard, we are in the heart of Los Angeles. See this group of ours, this is all we have here. So by you saying that you are a Christian, then you are saying that you are alone. When they find out who you are, they are going to come after you. When that happens, don't come to us. We know all about your case. We know you fought your case straight up and didn't turn, for that you earned our respect. If you want to follow Jesus here, then do it. If we find out you are fake and hiding behind a bible... well, that is going to be an issue. This is a low-level yard, so you can do what you want. But if this was a level two... you would have had a knife in you for what you just said. So, good luck bro and watch your back." When he finished speaking, he walked off and half of the group left with him. A few lingered to shake my hand and asked questions about the jails I was in. After a few minutes, I walked off to where Jacobo was at.

"Brother David, is everything okay?" looking concerned.

"Yes brother, everything is okay," I answered.

By this time, the next movement was about to happen. Jacobo said we need to make our way back to the unit so we can talk and meet with one of the other brothers. As we walked back I thanked God for protecting me and giving me the words to speak. Survival in prison always comes down to words. How you conduct yourself and how you speak to others. Knowing how to communicate and carry yourself will take you a long way in prison. With two years of conditioning and also being schooled in the streets, I knew I would be able to hold my own.

Once it was evening, Jacobo came by my bunk where I was relaxing.

"It's time for service brother," He said.

"Service? At the chapel on a weekday?" I asked confused.

"No brother, we have service every night in the yard. Get ready for movement, it's time for you to meet the brothers," said Jacobo with the biggest smile I've ever seen on an inmate. He reminded me of the Jack in the Box bobblehead guy with his huge smile.

We made our way to the yard for the evening. There was a huge wave of inmates from other units making their way to the yard. Many had been at work all day or in the unit. The evening was when everyone came out. Once we made it to the south yard, we began approaching a few benches by the basketball courts. I saw a group of twelve men gathered already. They all turned to embrace Jacobo. Before I had a chance to introduce myself, Jacobo began to speak to them all.

"This is brother David. He just came in today, he lives in my unit. He loves Jesus and is our brother!"

And for the first time in two years, I received hugs, smiles, and handshakes. They all rejoiced in meeting me. I forgot I was in a prison, it could have been in a church parking lot. These men didn't have the faces of men doing time. They were joyful, happy and genuinely glad to meet me. By the time I greeted each of them, there were now over fifteen men there gathered in a circle. The shortest of the group then motioned for everyone to get in a circle, they all listened. Mario was dark, stocky and had the demeanor of a pastor filled with the Holy Ghost. He began to speak.

"Hello brothers, God bless you all. We are here once again to worship God. I thank Him for sending David to us. Brother, you are welcome here. We

169

gather here each evening to pray together, sing together and preach together. Each night one of the brothers shares a Word from God. We rotate, so that way they can learn and be ready when they leave this place. Before we go into prayer, would you like to say anything?"

His eyes were like fire as he looked at me. I hadn't sensed the Spirit of God so strongly in someone since I was a child, going to church with my parents. I looked at each of the brothers as they waited for me to speak. I couldn't hold it any longer and tears began to fall down my face.

"I... I prayed for a day like this. I have been in a cell for two years. I have been in solitary for the past year. I begged God for a brother to share with. I begged God to allow me to hear worship. I begged God for someone to show me songs I can learn that worship Him. I can't believe I am here! I can't believe that I am out of my cell and standing out in the open with the sky above me and the smell of the ocean." I couldn't say any more words. I was overwhelmed with God's goodness.

Mario said a few more words and brother Chuy began leading worship. No instruments, no beautiful voices, just the men clapping. Men that love Jesus singing at the top of their lungs for all to hear. I raised up my hands, closed my eyes and soaked in the moment. Thank you, Lord, thank you. You have answered my prayers and given me more than what I deserve.

12

THE DAY SIR DYNO DIED

I fell right into place in Terminal Island. I was able to use the skills I learned from pencil drawing in the hole to make extra income drawing portraits for people. Stamps and food items were considered a currency. The prison was its own society with its own currency, rules, code of ethics and discipline. If you wanted a haircut, a barber would charge a few tuna pouches or stamps. Some would do laundry service for a certain amount of commissary each week. Others would shine boots and iron clothes to perfection for those receiving visits during the weekend. Chefs that owned restaurants and were doing time for tax evasion would cook meals with commissary, food taken from the kitchen and a microwave that would rival any restaurant. In the same way, a city is full of people going back and forth from work, running errands, going to the gym, going to school or church. It was the exact same way in prison, besides the fact that we were a small eco-system of society that couldn't leave.

The leader of the group, Mario, sat down with me on my second day in prison. He took the time to hear my story, much in the same way a pastor would sit down with a new visitor to the church. He sat with patience as I shared all I had been through with gangs, drugs, music, and solitary. I asked about his life and he openly shared with me his own life story. Over the next few months, this man Mario, a convict with no credentials became my pastor. I listened to every word he preached when it was his turn to preach. I sat next to him just to hear what he would teach over lunch or dinner. Sometimes a small group of us would sit at a table and open our Bibles with him as he poured wisdom out of every verse we read. I took note of how he carried himself when there was a conflict between brothers or a non-believer with one of the brothers. I never mentioned my calling to preach as we gathered in the yard each evening for one of the brothers in the group to preach. I'd show up in the yard in the evening with my Bible in hand to worship then learn. All of those months I had to myself with no preacher, pastor or sermons. Now I was overdosing with a sermon every night. I soon realized that there were other groups of Christians, almost like different denominations. Yet we were friendly, and on Sunday all of the groups would fill the chapel when the chaplain would preach with a full service that included a worship team and musicians.

Three months had passed by when Mario wanted to talk with me. He pulled me to the side.

"David, I would like you to preach on Thursday," he asked with a warm smile.

I felt nervous yet ready. It was the confirmation I had been waiting for. I had continued writing my sermons and sending them to my parents. Mario asking me to preach felt like Billy Graham asking me. I was humbled.

"Okay, I'm ready. Thank you for the opportunity," I said.

"I know that you will do great, brother," said Mario.

I felt so excited and began writing my sermon within the same hour that he asked me. When the day finally arrived, I had my notes, certain parts I made sure to highlight with my marker. It was going to be explosive and anointed, I was sure of it. I had so many powerful points, I just knew it was going to blow their minds. I literally felt as if the entire prison yard was going to stop what they were doing just to come to hear. The points were that good! During the time of prayer and worship, I couldn't concentrate, I was too excited thinking about how great it would be to finally follow my calling to preach.

Once worship was over, all of the men of the group sat down at the two picnic tables to face Mario as he stood up to welcome them for coming. The way Mario spoke at the two tables, was as if he was in a huge church speaking to hundreds of men, women, and children. He let everyone know that he had asked me to preach. All of the brothers clapped with encouragement as I walked up to stand behind the garbage can that was used each evening as a pulpit. The top of the lid was flat, so it was perfect to hold a bible and notes. I looked up and saw twelve faces looking at me. I prayed and laid my notes next to my Bible. I felt the anointing ready to pour and the Holy Spirit begin to stir, but the wind also stirred and my notes went flying. Some of the brothers quickly jumped to help me gather them, which took a few seconds to get them back and put them back in order. I felt nervous and looked at Mario. He simply smiled and motioned for me to keep going.

It wasn't coming out the way I imagined it. I continuously lost my place, I had too many pages for the sermon and felt rushed to deliver it all. I skipped parts, repeated others. It was a complete disaster. By the time I finished, I was glad it was over. My preaching days were done. The brothers clapped, most likely out of pity. The bell rang for final movement back to the units and I gathered my Bible and notes and quickly tried to walk away from shame. All of these months feeling as if God had truly called me to preach, I had made a mistake. The weight was heavy on my shoulders, I would never be able to preach for God. When I got back to my unit, I showered and laid down, playing the sermon over and over in my head. In my mind it was powerful, but I couldn't get it out of my mouth in the same way I heard it in my head.

The next day after lunch I ran into Mario.

"Hello brother David, God bless you," he said.

"...I'm really sorry about last night. I know you expected me to preach better. I don't know what happened," I quickly said.

"Brother, it's okay. I want you to preach again next week."

I looked at him feeling confused. "What do you mean preach again? I can't preach! You saw what happened! I can't preach like you or the other brothers."

"David, you will do better next week. Matter of fact, I want you to preach every week from now on.

It is time that you operate in your calling. I know you have it in you. Don't try to preach like me or anyone else. Preach like David. Preach in the way God is calling you to preach. Okay?" he asked.

I hesitated, thinking he must be crazy. I didn't want to let him down, so I accepted. He was my friend and my pastor and I did not want to let him down.

Every other week a pastor would come in as a visitor to preach on a Tuesday night. This was the only night we didn't gather in the yard. He would come to the chapel and share a powerful word. His name was Fermin Campos from Los Angeles. He was a Pentecostal pastor that preached with so much passion and fire, I quickly realized that Fermin was a mentor to Mario. This fact made me instantly respect and receive the powerful sermons and teachings that Fermin brought.

From the moment I arrived in Terminal Island, I inquired about water baptism. I had sent request after request to the chaplains in Sacramento County Jail and Santa Rita. Neither of them was allowed or had the facilities for water baptisms. By this time I was now over two years in Christ, yet not able to be baptized. It was something I yearned for, ever since I read the book of Acts, and how the Ethiopian greatly desired to be baptized.

Acts 8:36-38 New King James Version

36 Now as they went down the road, they came to some water. And the eunuch said, "See, here is water. What hinders me from being baptized?" 37 Then Philip said, "If you believe with all your heart, you may." And he answered and said, "I believe that Jesus Christ is the Son of God." 38 So he commanded the chariot to stand still. And both Philip and the eunuch went down into the water, and he baptized him.

The day finally arrived that the chaplain gave permission for Fermin to baptize me and a handful of other brothers. That day, the baptismal tub was taken out, cleaned up and filled in the lobby of the chapel. All was set, besides waiting for Fermin to arrive in the evening. I had waited for twenty-eight months for this moment. I called my parents to let them know the good news.

I anxiously waited for the phone to be answered. My mom answered and I instantly knew something was wrong.

"What's wrong mom!"

"Mijo, you know your tia Benny has been sick... she just passed away."

My heart dropped in my chest, I felt like I couldn't breathe. She was my aunt that always spoke life into me. She was the one that rejoiced when she found out I was serving God in prison. She was like a mother to me. The prayer warrior that refused to give up. Now she was gone. I began to weep as my mom continued to try to encourage me. What kind of nephew was I? stuck here in this prison for my dumb decisions and couldn't even be there with her in her last days. After everything she did for me, I couldn't even be there. After a few minutes, we said our goodbyes. This was a day I had been waiting for, now it was a day I wanted to forget. I sat on my bunk motionless as I scrolled my mind of so many memories. Times as a child she cooked for me, talked with me, encouraged me and prayed for me. Our talks as I grew up to be a teenager, then as an adult. I would never get a chance to see her again.

After a few hours, one of the brothers came to get me for the baptism. I had no drive in me to even walk, yet I made my way to the chapel. A small group of us gathered around the portable baptismal as Fermin spoke and shared scriptures. I watched him baptize the first brother, then the second brother. I was next. I felt so numb. When he baptized the first two brothers, he spoke to them a few words of what baptism meant and said a short prayer for each of them. I was nudged, letting me know I was next. I looked at Fermin as Mario stood right next to him. I stepped into the baptismal and I could no longer hold my tears. I cried for the pain of the last two years, I cried for all of my sins that I had committed against God. I cried for my Tia that would not be there anymore. I cried for my family. I cried for the fact that I waited so many months for this moment to happen, and now here I was before God. I wanted to give Jesus my all, this was my final proclamation to Him that I belonged to Him and Him alone.

Fermin began to pray over me in a way that reminded me of the pastors of my youth.

"Lord Jesus, I pray for an anointing over David like never before. You give him the words and the strength to speak for You with a fire like never before. I pray for the multitudes that he will reach for your name's sake. I pray for Your Spirit to dwell in him so powerfully that demons will run!" Then he turned to me.

"David look at me." I looked up with tears streaming down my face.

"Do you proclaim Jesus to be the King of your life, the Savior of your soul?"

I nodded yes.

"Do you surrender your entire life and vow to follow Jesus with all of your heart?"

I nodded yes.

"David, according to Scripture, I baptize you in the powerful name of Jesus. When you go down, you are dying to your old self. And when I bring you up, you are coming up a new man. Your old man will stay in these waters, and you will be a new man."

I held my wrist, and with the other hand, held my nose. The last words I heard before going back into the water were, "In Jesus' name."

Once I was pushed back into the water I shot up like a rocket. As if struck by electricity. My arms went up and I began to shout, I tried to shout praises in English but my tongue was speaking in a way I had never heard before. This was different than what happened in my cell in solitary. I felt free, I felt liberated. I felt the power of God. I felt His comfort in my broken heart because of my tia. I knew without a shadow of a doubt that my tia was alive and rejoicing for me in heaven. Chains were broken and shattered. I was speaking in tongues at the top of my lungs. The chaplain came out of his office and began to rejoice with us. I stepped out of the water as the brothers all hugged me and the other two brothers that were also baptized. Mario came last and gave me a hug. He didn't say a word but his smile said much. It was June 6th, 2006. A day I will never forget.

I hesitantly continued to preach each week, and just like Mario said, it got easier each time. I felt more open to sharing with the other brothers some of the things I learned in the Scriptures while in solitary. We would all have breakfast together, lunch together, some of us would exercise or lift weights together. Each evening we would have worship and preaching. I had learned a lot about the bible while in a cell, but now I had the opportunity to live it out in a group setting with other believers and non-believers.

One night during service out in the yard, it was Mario's turn to preach. We had our regular typical worship time, but instead of Mario preaching, he began to give a prophetic word to each of us. One by one he prayed over us with such intense prayer that all I could do was bow my head and receive all he was saying to me and to the others. It was so out of the ordinary for him. It wouldn't make sense why it was different, until the next day.

The next morning I was awakened by the noise of the prison being put on lockdown. We were so accustomed to getting out for breakfast and starting our day. Everyone was at the door of the unit wondering why the guards weren't opening up. Every unit in the prison was locked down. Then word got around that a whole bunch of inmates were transported in the middle of the night. It was random, and as far as we knew, it was for no reason. Chuy, Mauro and I began to get worried. What if some of the brothers were sent off? We were in the same unit, but the other brothers lived in the various units. Finally, after two hours, we were let out.

Each brother from every unit instinctively went to the south yard to our tables. One by one everyone began to show up. We all greeted each other, yet, also worried if anyone else was missing. After a few minutes, every single brother was accounted for except Mario. Within a few minutes, someone from Mario's unit came to tell us that Mario was taken along with fifty other inmates. No reason was given. Later we found out that inmates were taken from various prisons in order to fill up an empty one in the Bakersfield area. I was devastated, we all were. We sat at our table in complete silence. We all felt like sheep with no shepherd. Some of the brothers left the table with heads down, back to their units. Those that stayed talked about the night before. How did Mario know to pray for us? It would be our last service with him, and the Holy Spirit led him to anoint and prophesy to each of us individually. By the next movement, the few that remained at the table left. I didn't want to go back to my unit. I decided to stay there alone. I put on my sunglasses so nobody would notice any tears. After all of my time in prison with no one to lead me, nobody to pour into me, and now he was gone. What was our group going to do now? There is nobody fit to lead this group without Mario. Would we all fall apart? So many things were going through my mind.

I began to reflect again in my past life. Here I was in federal prison. How did all of this happen so quickly? Exactly how my tia Benny prophesied back when she called me. She said that satan would take me high up a mountain, and I would think that I was at my peak. Then once I was at the top, the devil was going to kill me and throw me off of the mountain. My music career led me down a dark path. I rubbed shoulders with killers that had no remorse. The company I kept was a who's who in many prison gang documentaries. Yet I couldn't stop the rollercoaster. Now here once again was another unstoppable rollercoaster. It was a different ride, but also uncontrollable. We could be here one minute and transported to another state for no reason. Our phone calls were limited to fifteen minutes with only three hundred minutes allowed each month. What is ironic is the fact that many come to prison in the first place because they don't like to be corrected, or ordered. Yet our entire life in prison is controlled. Where to sleep, when to eat, what to eat, what to wear, when we could walk, and where we could walk. Not only did we have to live according to the rules of the prison officials, but we also have to live or die by the rules of the inmates. You could be sentenced to a few years, but because of situations that are out of your control, you could catch more time. Your release date was not written in stone, it was merely a suggestion. This is the life I chose, so how could I sit here and complain about Mario being taken. In my heart of hearts I know that I deserve this prison sentence. I deserve to be sitting here on this bench. I deserve all that I suffered in solitary confinement. We all deserve what we have coming to us. But God...

13

PREACH LIKE IT WAS 10,000 PEOPLE

All-day long we were all in prayer for the direction of our group. Mario was taken along with fifty other inmates. We were all going to individually pray and come back in the evening for service in the south yard. We would then discuss our future to see what the Lord was telling each of us. I had no idea who would lead us now, especially because I didn't know the guys as much as they knew each other. I was the newest addition to the group. I simply prayed for all of the men to be in one accord and I would simply follow. Mario held the group together in a way I had never seen done before, along with having respect from all of the population no matter what race or beliefs they had.

In the evening I was the last one to arrive at the tables. Everyone was already sitting down and talking. My heart still felt heavy at the loss. Chuy welcomed me, as well as the other brothers. I sat down with them waiting for them to begin to discuss our future. Chuy began with prayer which was normal since he always led worship for our evening services. Once the prayer was over he looked directly at me.

"David, we have all been in prayer. We've been praying for brother Mario and his safety. We've all been praying about a new leader for our group."

I nodded. "That's all I've been doing also brother," I said.

Chuy continued. "Each of these men has been in prayer and we have all come to the same exact conclusion."

'Wow', I thought to myself. How amazing that God had already shown all of these men, individually, our new spiritual leader.

Chuy looked right at me and said the words that I completely didn't understand for the first few seconds. "The Lord is telling us that you are the new leader."

I wasn't expecting it. I shook my head. "No

brother, no. I'm new here, I don't even know you all the way you know each other. You all preach powerful sermons!"

Chuy smiled and looked at the other brothers. "Brother David, we would never force you. But please consider the fact that we are all in accord with what the Lord was telling each of us. You are a good brother, you know the bible and your heart is toward God. We need your leadership, it's time for you to step up into your calling. I will be by your side, we all will."

I hesitated for a second then nodded my head, "Okay, I accept it."

All of the brothers now smiled and began shaking my hand and hugging me. Was I afraid? Yes, I was, but afraid to lead God's people should always be in the list of emotions when taking on such an important role as a shepherd. This is more important than anything on earth, to watch, lead, correct and guide other souls into the Kingdom of God.

With Mario gone, I began to fill my day with Bible studies. I felt that it was important to teach individually so they could grow in their walk and understanding of Scripture. Then by evening, we would gather for evening service. I began to build a good relationship with the prison chaplain. The chapel was important for us because different ministries would send it VHS tapes of teachings and sermons. I began to book time almost daily with one of the tv's that were lined up in cubicles so I could watch and learn from other pastors.

Terminal Island offered the RDAP program, so I made an appointment with my counselor to get in right away. I figured it would be worth getting on the list now at the beginning of my sentence since I was told that there was a long list of inmates trying to be transferred to Terminal Island for the program. By my fifth month, I was called in to speak to the director of the RDAP program. I was surprised due to the fact that I knew I still had a lot of time to do. I walked over to the administrative office and was told to go into an office. A woman sat there looking at my paperwork. After a few minutes, she began to speak.

"Hello, David. I was looking over your request to enter the program. I see in your court papers that your judge recommended you for the RDAP program. You are on the top of the list since you will be releasing soon. It is a nine-month program, so you will be finishing right on time. By completing and graduating from the program, twelve months will be reduced from your sentence."

I was completely confused. "I'm sorry but did I hear you correctly? You said I will be releasing right after the program. I don't understand. I am serving a ninety-six-month sentence. I am not even halfway complete. I think there is a mistake in your paperwork. I shouldn't be releasing for another five years or so without the twelve-month reduction."

This time she looked confused and began re-reading through my paperwork.

"I'll get back to you. I will look deeper into this issue and will be calling on you to come back."

I thanked her and walked away. I knew it was a mistake. I talked to the brothers and they had never heard of anything like that happening. I ignored it and just fell right back into my daily program with the brothers. I continued preaching in the yard once a week and kept the same preaching rotation that Mario had started. By this time my preaching style was beginning to form and it began to get the attention of men that didn't belong to our group. At times we would have a gathering of non-believers listening to the gospel of Jesus Christ.

Once, I shared "If you are in Christ, you can be free from this place! We are in heavenly places through Christ Jesus according to Scripture."

One man spoke up. "What do you mean free from this place?"

I pointed in the direction of the ocean which could be seen from the south yard. "What do you see when you look in that direction?"

All of the men turned to look that way. He said, "I see fences, barbwire and a gun tower with a guard in it."

"That's interesting," I said. I continued, "When I look that direction I see a big ocean for miles, I see a dark blue sky. When I focus on the fence and barbwire, it makes the water blurry, but when I focus on the water, it makes the fence blurry. Almost to the point that it disappears. To be in Christ is to not be a part of this world. This prison can only lock up my flesh, not my mind or my heart. How you see this world is how you will live in it. I can drive for miles yet only see a short distance ahead of me, but if I fly in a plane, I am able to see as far as the horizon. So what is your perspective? If the Bible says that I am in heavenly places in Christ Jesus, that means my perspective has to change. How I see you, how I see myself and how I see my current situation in this prison. They can lock me in a cell and I will still be freer than I have ever been in all of my life."

The man walked away, he just couldn't see it. This was exactly why we are called to reach the lost. We were never called to condemn the lost, but to show them the light. And that light is Jesus Christ.

After a few days, I was called back to speak to the director of the RDAP program. I was told that I would be enrolled in the next program and to pack my locker to move into the residential unit for RDAP which was only a few doors away from the unit I was staying at. She was persistent that no error was found in my release date and that I would be released as soon as I finished the program. I tried to hand her my own paperwork, showing my sentence date but she would not listen. I decided to stop arguing the point and just get the program over with. That way when they did find the mistake, I would now have a twelve-month reduction in my sentence. To be in the RDAP, it meant that you were housed with your classmates for the entirety of the nine months. We met in a classroom for a few hours each day as the teacher broke into our minds in a way that has helped me in my life. We not only learned about addiction but behavior, thinking errors, how the mind works and how we interact with each other. We learned lessons on communication and using cognitive and critical thinking instead of being impulsive. We would watch Hollywood movies, but with lessons attached to them that helped me see movies in a different light. We learned about the downward spiral that many take but don't notice until it's too late. We learned our triggers in our personality that would help us or hinder us in our future relationships with spouse, children, family, and friends. I believe that when RDAP is taken seriously, it can change and alter a mindset for the better in any person. I learned more about myself through RDAP than I ever have in my life. Even surpassing things I learned in solitary because even though solitary showed me who I really was, RDAP helped explain who I was. By the end of the nine-month program, all of the class asked me to be the speaker at the small graduation with the warden, assistant warden, and staff and classmates. I knew that it was great while it lasted, yet I also knew that they would find the mistake on my release date. Anytime someone graduated RDAP, someone in headquarters for Federal Burea of Prisons would recalculate your prison sentence with the twelve-month reduction. I was sure it would now be caught and adjusted correctly.

The next day after graduating I was called into my counselors' office. I was given my release papers and told to communicate with my family to let them know the time and day to pick me up. Once again I tried to explain that it was a mistake. By this time, word had gotten around back home and to my old friends that I was getting out, which made no sense to anyone because they knew I had seven and a half years to serve. The counselor would not listen to me and gave me boxes so I could clean out my locker so I could take my property with me. I called home and explained that even though I know it's a mistake, the prison was going to release me the following morning. There was nothing I could do and nobody I could talk to. I was being forced to leave. To this day I have no idea what happened. During our evening service, we spend it in prayer and fellowship. No matter what I thought, I was going to have to leave. I said my goodbyes to the brothers as I made my way back to the unit. My children back home were excited, dad was finally coming home. I decided to just roll with it. Either this was a God thing, or a mistake and I would be re-arrested sooner or later. It was not how I wanted to live, but I couldn't force the prison to keep me.

As I sat on my bunk, the correctional officer walked up to me.

"Rocha, your counselor wants to talk to you."

I knew it. I shook my head and made my way to his office. I knocked and when he motioned for me to walk in, I did and sat down.

He looked at me and said, "David, unfortunately, there's been a mistake. We re-calculated your sentence and you still have to serve two and a half more years with the RDAP adjustment."

"Sir, I've told you this from the beginning and nobody would listen. You had me call my parents and family. They will be on their way to get me in a few hours because it's a seven-hour drive for them. I've told my children that I am coming home. You had probation go to my house to approve the place of residence," I said with less frustration than what I was feeling.

"Well, I'm sorry this happened. Would you like to use the phone?"

"Yes, please," I answered.

I picked up the phone and dialed my parent's home phone. I knew my children would be there along with their mother. They were preparing for the trip to pick me up. When I told them the news I could hear everyone in tears. I couldn't hold it and tears fell down my face. I knew that day broke the hearts of my children. It would be the beginning of the end of my relationship with their mother, the time was just too long to wait.

By the next day, everyone in the prison knew what happened. Inmates I had never talked to, came to say they were sorry about the mistake. How could something like this happen? The southside OG that spoke to me in the beginning and helped me get a haircut gave me words of encouragement. As I walked the yard the next day, I was approached by the shot-caller for the northerners. He had never spoken or acknowledged me since the day I approached them on my first day. He had something in his hand.

"David," he said.

I turned toward him. "Hey,"

"I want to talk with you for a minute... I want you to have this," it was a black leather Bible. "I heard about what happened. That's not cool at all bro. I have watched you since you arrived here and I just want to say that you have my respect. You are real about what you believe and I just want to let you know. I have this Bible in my locker and I don't read it. Maybe it would be better with you."

I took the Bible from his hand and shook his hand.

"I appreciate it, man. I know the rules and repercussions of this life we live in. So I thank you and appreciate all you could have done but didn't," I said wholeheartedly.

"No problem brother, again, I'm sorry about what happened to you. I'm sure your family was heartbroken."

I looked down as I imagined my children. "Yeah, it's not even about me. I can bounce back. It's my kids' man."

Then he walked away back to the group of homies.

Every day for lunch each counselor and the

warden would stand outside of the chow hall. This time as I stood in line for chow, the warden walked up to me along with an officer. I had never spoken with the warden in my entire stay. I figured it was smart to just do my time and stay below the radar from any staff.

The warden was thin and tall. He always wore a sharply tailored suit.

"Mr. Rocha...."

"Yes, that's me," I answered.

"Can I have a word with you. You aren't in trouble," he reassured.

I looked at the brothers that I with as we stood in line.

"Sure," I said and followed them a few steps away from the line.

The warden began to speak. "I just want to apologize on behalf of our staff in not finding this mistake. I was informed that you had been telling my staff since the beginning. I don't understand how this happened.

I began to speak. "Sir, I am here to serve my time, there is nothing I can do about that. But to force me out of here, force me to call my family and give hope to my children was cruel to them. My sons were marking off on the calendar for the day I would come home."

"David, again I am sorry. Is there anything I can do within my power?"

I did not hesitate and quickly said, "I want to be closer to home."

"Where is home?" he asked.

"Tracy, up north. There is a federal prison camp in Atwater, less than an hour away. I am camp eligible and graduated from RDAP."

He nodded his head in deep thought. Then he called over my counselor who was standing a few feet away. When the counselor reached us, the warden began giving him instructions.

"I want you to pull Mr. Rocha's file. See if he is camp eligible. If so, let's get him transferred immediately."

The counselor didn't like it. There was protocol for going to camp. Before anyone left Terminal Island for camp, they first had to work as part of the landscape crew that worked outside of the prison grounds for six months. Then after that, the counselor would process the paperwork that usually took about two or three months, then the long wait for transporting the inmate. All together it was about a ten to twelve-month process. The counselor walked away and the warden looked back toward me.

"Rocha, if he does not get back to you within two

days, please let me know. Go ahead and get back in line, I don't want you to miss your dinner."

"Thank you, I appreciate it," I said as I walked back into line where the brothers were waiting for me.

Once again, the Lord showed me that He can open any door He so pleases. He guides the hearts of kings like rivers, going any which way that God pleases.

Proverbs:21:1 *The king's heart is in the hand of the Lord,*

Like the rivers of water;

He turns it wherever He wishes.

The brothers rejoiced with me at the fact that I was going to be transferred closer to home. It was a bitter-sweet moment knowing that I was leaving an amazing group of believers. Terminal Island proved to be a place of growth. Even though I had no freedom, in the sense of a civilian, I was able to grow spiritually into the man I would be in the future. The group had grown under my leadership and I was allowed to preach on a Sunday service in the chapel. The chaplain trusted me and that meant a lot to me. I had taken so many brothers under my wing, like Josue who has stayed my friend for years now. Upon leaving, I left the group in the hands of Chuy and blessed him with that leadership.

A few weeks later I was not only being transferred,

but I was given a furlough transfer. Which meant that family could pick me up and take me to Atwater. I was given fifteen hours to get to a destination that was only six hours away. This was unheard of, yet God opened the doors. I know it wasn't as good as going home, but I was able to spend time with my children and family for a few hours in the free world before I turned myself into the prison camp to finish my last two and a half years.

14

ATWATER, WHERE I LEARNED TO TALK WITH JESUS

I woke up at 5 am that morning and told to walk into the front office. I was checked for Identification and buzzed in. It was cold and the sun hadn't risen yet. I was given papers and told that I better show up at Atwater by 7 pm. Just like that, I was outside the gate. I had planned my trip with brother Josue's mother. She pastored a church literally fifteen minutes away from the prison. When she found out I was given a furlough to camp, she gladly accepted to take me as far as Bakersfield, a three-hour drive. Once we made it to Bakersfield, I met with my children and their mother. I thanked Josue's mother and we drove off heading north. The entire plan was to get to Atwater with enough time to see my parents and family. They were waiting at a local park as we drove up. I was able to sit with my children and watch them play. We ate sandwiches and chips like a regular picnic. To be with family after the past few years felt like I died and went to heaven. I wanted time to slow down so I wouldn't have to turn myself into custody. We laughed, we cried and talked. Before we knew it, my time was up. I had to walk myself back into prison for two years and some change.

I walked into the prison to be booked not one minute early or late. I was given clothes, boots, a blanket, and a pillow as a guard walked with me out of the high-level penitentiary to the prison camp next door. As I approached the camp I realized there was no fence around the complex and no barbed wire. The entire camp was two big metal buildings, one as the living quarters for up to 110 men, and the other building for cafeteria, classrooms, chapel, visiting, commissary and library. The second I walked into the open dorm a Chicano asked me where I was from. I told him I was a Christian from Tracy. He walked away and within a few minutes, another man approached me with a care package.

"They tell me you're a Christian," said the man. "I'm Larry, I'm a brother also."

"Amen," I shook his hand and he led me to where my bunk would be. He introduced me to a handful of other brothers as I settled in. I recognized one of the northerners that was in Terminal Island when I first approached them there. He came up and welcomed me. I quickly learned that there was no Bible study groups, no fellowship at all whatsoever. The Chaplain would come from the main prison to preach on Sunday morning and disappear until the following Sunday. For the next few days, I began to ask questions as I sat with brother Larry. He explained that there was a big Christian group, but the man that held it together was transferred out to a different prison and soon after division came and the group fell apart. Since then it was only himself, brother Nacho and brother Mario, who only spoke Spanish. This was a different Mario than the leader we had in Terminal Island. Most of the time there was no correctional officer at the camp to watch us. There was trust, the officials knew that nobody wanted to lose their freedom and get sent to a higher level. It would have been easy to simply walk off and never come back, but for most, we were at the end of our sentence. It would have made no sense to escape and be a federal fugitive. Each evening at

6 pm I would go outside to walk the track alone. I knew that the brothers in Terminal Island would be gathered at the tables. I began to miss them. I would sing worship songs I had learned from Chuy. If I couldn't be with them in person, I knew I was with them in spirit. At 7 pm I would take out my Bible and read for the entire hour. It was a program that was instilled in me with daily fellowship. I couldn't live with just Sunday morning service. The best part of being in Atwater was being able to see my children and my family each and every week. In Terminal Island, I was only able to see my children and family maybe three times. Yet my spiritual life was feeling stagnant. I soon learned that the classrooms that were used for GED classes during the day were open and available during the evenings. I decided that I would sit in a classroom each evening at 6 pm to study my bible. I wouldn't invite anyone, I would just do what I did with the brothers in Terminal Island. Things had to be shaken up and the gospel had to be preached.

After a few days of sitting alone for an hour each day, brother Larry came around looking for me. I explained to him that I would study each day for one hour. He decided to join me. Within a few weeks, we had a handful of men each day with Bible in hand. The group began to form, unity took place and God blessed it. Larry, Randy, Nacho, Mario and myself. Then brother Johnny was transferred and joined the group. Also, brother Lorenzo and Edwin. We would study entire books of the Bible, we studied church history, apologetics, theology. We began inviting men to Sunday service and helped Chaplain Weaver give structure to each service. We would each give an offering of hygiene products as a way to give each new arrival a care package. No matter what race or whether they were believers or not. It was a powerful way to share the love of Christ. This idea of a care package was established long before I arrived, but it was something that grew stronger with a newly united group of brothers. I was assigned a job in the commissary warehouse, along with brother Johnny. This allowed us to fellowship throughout the day. I soon learned about a Bible University that was willing to give courses to inmates at a reduced price. I enrolled and quickly began deepening my studies as a student of CLU (Christian Leadership University).

The first required course was titled: How to hear God's voice. In the beginning, I thought it was a cool catchy title until I began to read the first chapter. It explained how God was always talking, we just never listened long enough to know His voice. It taught about the four keys to hearing God's voice.

- Key #1 God's voice is spontaneous. Learn to discern it.
- Key #2 Quiet yourself, learn to still your mind.
- Key #3 Envision what you are hearing.
- Key #4 Journal and write down what you see and hear

At the end of chapter one is given an exercise to do before going onto the next lesson. It required that I write a letter to Jesus, not a list of things I wanted from Him, just a simple few sentences of what He meant to me. Then I was to quiet myself, envision with the eyes and ears of my heart and write down what I felt He was saying to me. I was very hesitant and put my book away for the next two days. I didn't know how this could possibly work. I had prayed every single day since my incarceration, yet I never stopped to actually listen. It was always a one-way conversation. Of course, I felt His presence, of course, I knew He was with me. Dozens of times I felt Him nudging me to take certain directions or to speak to a certain person. Yet, I never actually stopped to see if He had anything to say to me.

The push to try the letter grew heavier and heavier on my heart. I had a night light in my locker next to my bunk. When the lights went out I decided I would give it a try. I simply told Jesus that I loved Him and I thanked Him for being with me during all of this time. I then put my pencil down to see if I heard anything with the ears of my heart. The instructions were to write down the first spontaneous thing that came to your mind. Don't analyze it, don't try to figure it out, just simply write it all down. Once it was written you can go over it for as long as you'd like. I began to hear within myself, words. Not like myself speaking to myself, but as if a person talking to me. I began to write it down. The words were so full of compassion and love. The way He began to describe me and what I meant to Him. I continued to write as I felt the words pouring into my very soul. My eyes watered and dropped down onto the page. Here I was, praying to Him for over three years, and He was actually answering. The floodgates of communication were wide open and I couldn't stop the voice even if I tried. Like a flood pouring onto dry dusty land. I knew from that moment that I would never be the same again. My prayer life would never be the same. There were some major landmarks in my Christian life. The day I surrendered, the day I was baptized in the Holy Spirit, the day I was baptized in water by Pastor Fermin, and this moment right now.

It only took me one month to finish the college course and was ready for another one. I decided that I would work toward an associate in Biblical studies which was sixty credits. I knew that I had to prepare myself for ministry once I was released. What better way than to build a strong Biblical foundation. I needed to understand my Bible if I was going to grow and help others. I no longer looked at my remaining sentence as a heavy burden. Atwater prison camp became my Bible college, and I was simply a student away from home.

15

I WILL BUILD A HOUSE OF REST FOR THE ARK OF THE COVENANT

With the Bible college lessons, the first year in Atwater passed quickly. Our group was strong and we were all learning. Visits from my parents, aunts, and my brothers continued weekly. I knew something was wrong when visits with my children and their mother became further and further apart. It was now February of 2008, exactly four years since my incarceration. The relationship ended like most relationships end with one person incarcerated. Time causes distance, and distance causes one to learn to live without the partner. Out of sight out of mind. My entire focus for the past four years was to get back to the family I had and raise my children. With the last tail end of my sentence left to go, I completely felt derailed. I didn't know how to deal with the abandonment, yet God gave me the strength to push forward. My parents began to bring my children every other week and that helped me in ways I could never describe.

Everything the devil did was to try to destroy me. From active gang members in Sacramento County Jail to a year in solitary confinement, then an assassin that was ordered to kill me yet the Lord pulled the killer into the Kingdom of God. Then I lost two of my aunts one month apart which were my dad's only sisters. Then I was told I would be released and it devastated my children and family when I wasn't. And now the last thread of hope of raising my children together in the house I purchased before incarceration fell through my hands. I was not going to let the devil break me. I had come too far for that. The enemy should have destroyed me a long time ago. I dove deeper and harder into my studies. I knew that if the enemy wanted to break my will that bad, then that meant that God had something special for my life. Everything the enemy tells you is a lie. If he tells you that you are nothing, then that means you are something. If he tells you that you can't fix the issue, then that means through Christ it can be fixed.

I began to walk the track at night after Bible study just to get my head straight. I began to have conversations with God as I walked. Journaling became an everyday exercise. I learned to hear His voice in everything I did. I began to teach and operate as Jesus whispered the very sermons into my ear and I would deliver it. When the chaplain couldn't make it on a Sunday morning, we will still have service and I would deliver the Word. We would get visits from a pastor every other week in the middle of the week, and he would preach with a fire I had never seen since pastor Fermin Campos back in Terminal Island. We called him pastor Mike. He always made sure to bring a musician to lead worship. Sometimes it was a keyboardist, other times a guitarist. Pastor Mike began leading men into the baptism of the Holy Spirit with the evidence of speaking in tongues.

Chaplain Weaver approved to get a projector into the chapel and was given a budget for Christian films. We began to get catalogs from Christian Bible Distributors, and we would write a list of the DVD movies we wanted. We used the films to create a Christian movie night as a way to evangelize to the men in the unit. We would print up fliers and pass them out. We would gather our commissary and order snacks for everyone that came in to watch the movie. We would hook up the DVD player into the PA system and projected the movies onto a white wall, making the chapel feel like a movie theater. Some of the brothers that worked in the kitchen would get permission to bake cookies and cakes for the weekly event. All of the seats would be lined up with an aisle down the middle. Before playing the movie, we would show the movie trailer for next week's movie. Everyone loved it. We would begin in prayer and we would always share a quick five minute Scripture with an explanation that had to do with the film. Within a few weeks, each movie night was completely packed. It was a good escape for the men to watch a movie with a giant screen.

As the months were getting closer to my release, I still would have days of brokenness. There were times I would have nightmares of solitary. Other times I would have dreams of being free and walking around in a department store shopping, only to wake up on my bunk. I had no idea if I was going to be single for the rest of my life. Would I be alone? Who would want to be with an ex-convict with nothing to show. Before being arrested I owned my own home and had plenty of money with a rising career in the music and movie industry. Now I had nothing to offer to anyone and no home to live in once I was released. One night I fell asleep as I prayed, feeling completely defeated. I drifted off and the Lord gave me a dream.

I was walking into a big building with double doors. The music was loud and each seat was filled to capacity. Arms were raised and everyone was singing and worshipping. I began to slowly walk up the middle aisle toward the stage. I looked down at myself and noticed I was wearing shiny dress shoes and a suit. In the dream, I realized that I was the pastor of this church. Then I looked up to the stage and saw a line of worship singers. Some were men and some were women. Then I looked at the last singer on the right and it was a woman. She was singing with all of her heart. The Spirit of God was powerful and the anointing of God was thick. There was something about the woman singing, so I tried to focus on her face and it was a blur. No matter what I tried, I could not focus on her face. Each of the other singers were crystal clear. Within the dream, I asked God,

"Who is she, Lord?"

Then I heard within myself the voice of Jesus. "She is your wife."

And I woke up instantly. I sat up on my bed and realized I was in my bunk. Why did I dream that?

Where was this place? Who was the woman? Why was her face blurry? I had so many questions. I had fallen asleep broken, and now this dream somehow gave me hope. It was a vision of a future time, I knew it and received it. I wouldn't be alone in ministry. God was going to honor His promise of my calling and I would have the honor of pastoring a church for Him someday. That evening after Bible study I walked the track alone. This time, instead of talking with God, I began to pray about this mystery woman I saw in my dream. If God showed her to me, that means she existed. She was out there somewhere. I had no idea what her life was like or what she was going through.

I began to pray. "Lord, it's me again. I just thought I'd spend some time with you before heading into the unit. I want to pray for this woman you showed to me. Her face is blurry so I feel like it's someone I don't know yet. Whoever she is, wherever she is, please protect her. Watch over her and strengthen her. Bless her in all she does. Help her make the right decisions so we can find each other. I have no idea how to find her, but I know you will make a way for me. Thank you, Lord."

When I walked back into my unit, I decided to do something special. I laid on my bunk and pulled out my writing paper. I began to write this mystery woman a letter. I had no idea who she was or when I would meet her. I shared my heart with her and let her know I prayed for her on my walk. I also let her know that I would continue praying for her. At the end of the letter, I let her know that I would seal this letter until the day I handed it to her on our wedding day.

One of my ways to help make extra income while in Terminal Island was pencil drawing. By the time I made it to Atwater, I began learning how to paint with brushes using acrylic paint on canvas. I painted anything I got my hands on. Sports players, aquarium fish, portraits, landscapes, cartoons. Every day I would spend a few hours painting and honing my skills. One day the Lord kept impressing to me a design that he wanted me to draw out. It was now December of 2008 and I was busy with a long list of Christmas cards and portraits to do for some of the inmates. December was always a busy month as many of the men wanted paintings done as gifts to send home. Every day I was working to catch up, yet the Lord kept pushing me to draw a design out. I ignored it for three days. I continued to tell God that I would draw it out as soon as the holidays were over. God continued to push to the point that I would toss and turn at night when it was time to sleep. On the fourth day, I could no longer ignore it. On my way to work in the commissary warehouse, I took a drawing pad, a ruler and pens. Between work, I would take every chance I had to draw out what God was showing me. It was the design of a church building. A sort of blueprint. Where the doors would be, a small café or eatery, the classrooms, hallways, the bathrooms, the stage, and sanctuary. Rooms for meetings and storage. Every single detail of the building. When I got back to my unit from work, I showered and continued to draw the plans out. I couldn't stop, I didn't want to stop until I was finished. Once it was done I felt like I could finally breathe. The Lord spoke into my heart and said, 'This is going to be yours to further my kingdom. I told Noah to write out the plans for the ark, I told Moses to draw out the tabernacle and I continue to give my loved one's plans to draw out. I have never stopped planning.' I put the plans aside and continued back on my long list of projects for the different inmates.

On New Year's Eve, we were all in fellowship in one of the tv rooms. We wanted to enter into 2009 in prayer. I knew it would be my last year with these brothers. I was eligible to do my last six months in a halfway house in Oakland. Most inmates with no disciplinary reports, no violence on their records, no warrants in local counties, no sex crimes or molestation charges could finish off their sentence in a halfway house close to their home. It was a way to help the inmate transition back into society. You were allowed to find a job, have visits and build up enough trust to go home for the weekends. This meant that I would be leaving Atwater on July 27th, 2009. Right on my youngest son, David's birthday. When I was arrested he was only a toddler, now six years later, it would be his 9th birthday. My youngest daughter Aliyah was only one when I was arrested, Gabriel was five. I also had two older daughters, Angelyn and Liana who were now teenagers from my first marriage.

Once the new year hit, everyone in the unit began to go to their bunks to sleep. I laid down and dozed off talking to God. Once again the same recurring dream with me walking into the double doors. It was exactly like the first dream, yet within the dream, I knew I had been there before. This time I knew to focus on the worship singer. If there was some way to see her, but the blur was still there. Only this time as I was at the end of the dream I heard something different. I heard the words, 'House of Rest'. Then I woke up.

It was Jan 1st of 2009. New Year's day on a Thursday morning.

"House of Rest?" I said to myself as I sat up in my bed.

"Is that supposed to be the name of the church?" I asked myself. Since it was a holiday we didn't have work. So I spent my time in fellowship with brother Johnny, Lorenzo, and Edwin. I shared the name with them.

"It sounds like a funeral home to me," I said to them.

That evening I decided that I would find out once and for all if it was from God for the name of the church. I made a deal with the Lord.

"Jesus, House of Rest sounds like a funeral home. Like a place of rest. I don't know if this is from you or my imagination. I need confirmation Lord. So this is what I am going to do. I know it's highly unlikely, because I've never heard that term before, but I am going to look in my Bible concordance. If I can find that term in the Bible, then I know it's from you.

I reached into my locker and pulled out my Bible concordance. A Bible concordance is sort of like a dictionary. Every single word in the Bible is in alphabetical order, and along with the word is the Scripture locations that have that word within the verse. Also next to the word is a number code that leads to a definition in the back pages of the concordance. I opened the thick reference book and began to search. I could not believe my eyes when I saw the book reference this verse.

1 Chronicles 28:2

Then King David rose to his feet and said, "Hear me, my brethren and my people: I had it in my heart to build a house of rest for the ark of the covenant of the Lord, and for the footstool of our God, and had made preparations to build it.

My mouth dropped. Here it was, clear as day. In the Old Testament, King David wanted to build a permanent temple for the ark, which was a gold plated box with a lid. On top of the lid were two cherubims bowing and facing each other. The center of the lid was empty and representing the throne or seat of God. Inside of the box were the tablets of the commandments given to Moses, the rod used by his brother and a jar of manna. For years the ark of the covenant sat in a portable tent. King David wanted to honor God by building a temple, or a house for the ark to rest in. A House of Rest. In reading the rest of the chapter, King David felt compelled to draw out the plans for the temple, that way his son Solomon could build it. I knew at this point that the Lord had given me the name for the church I would pastor. I had no idea how to make it happen, nor did I know where it would be. What I did know is that it was going to happen, the promises of God do not go back to him void. What He promises, is what will come to pass.

Soon after the new year, I accomplished my first degree and immediately began working toward my Bachelor's degree. I also inquired to the Bible college about ordination. With letters of recommendation from various pastors I knew, including the chaplain and my perfect grades with the school I was honored to be ordained by the ordination branch of the university.

Before I realized, it was July and it was time for me to walk out of Atwater for my last six months to be served at the Oakland halfway house. The brothers had a huge going away party in the chapel and I prayed over brother Johnny to take over the group. I had made friends for life, my brothers. We had worshipped together, studied together, grew together and even cried together. Being in prison together created a bond that would never be broken. On the Monday morning of July 27th, 2009, my name was called on the buzzer to report to the main prison for release. I hugged the brothers one last time and walked out. I had no idea what the world was going to throw at me, but through Christ, I would withstand.

16

ONE MORE WAKE UP

'One more wake up' is a common saying in the prison system. When anyone became a short-timer, (a name given to someone getting close to being released) they would never count the day they were releasing. For instance, if it was a Sunday and your release day was Wednesday morning. You would say, "I got three days and a wake-up." On July 27th, my 'wake up' had finally arrived. I held a small box of my property and stood at the gate to wait. It had now been five and a half years since I had been free. I had no idea what waited for me outside of these gates. I wasn't technically free yet, I still had six remaining months of my sentence. In reality, I was still in custody and my family picking me up was simply a furlough transfer to the Oakland halfway house.

As I stood at the gate I had so many things running through my mind. I have spoken so many times to the brothers about this moment. Many times if a brother would stumble in their walk I would tell them. "If you are stumbling now... how are you going to handle the free world?" I had now been serving God since my incarceration, which had its own obstacles. But being in the free world had a whole other set of obstacles that I hadn't faced yet. How would I deal with enemies? How would I deal with finances and acclimating back into society? Where would I find other brothers in Christ? Can I still be a good father to my children after my long absence? Question after question. I began to pray.

"Lord, before I'm let out of this gate, I need you more than ever. I don't know how to live in the free world as a Christian. Please guide my steps. I don't want anything unless you give it to me. Watch over me and protect me. You are the only one that served this time with me. Open doors that need to be opened, and shut doors that need to be shut. In Jesus mighty name. Amen."

A correctional officer walked over, opened the gate and led me to the front of the penitentiary. As soon as my children saw me they ran out to me.

Today was my son's birthday, and as he hugged

me, he said, "Dad, today is my best birthday present ever!"

I hugged little David, my daughter Aliyah and my son Gabriel. Then I walked over and hugged my parents. And just like that, we got into the car and left the prison grounds. It was the oddest feeling. So much time had passed and yet it felt like it never happened as we drove further and further away from the prison. Someway, somehow I knew I would be okay.

As we drove through Tracy, the streets looked different. Everything looked different. We were given a little extra time to get to Oakland, and even though I wasn't supposed to stop anywhere, I wanted to see my parent's house. When we arrived, the house felt different, yet the peace of God was still very present the moment I walked in. Standing there in the living room with my parents and children around me. All of the time I was away overwhelmed me and I fell to my knees weeping. I was home. I knew I still had to finish my last six months, but I was home. No more cells, no more long corridors or handcuffs. It was behind me and I could be with my family. In the beginning, I thought my family would forget about me. I thought my children would see me as a stranger. God is faithful and good.

After a few minutes, we all loaded up into the car

again and made our way to Oakland. The halfway house was forty-five minutes away from Tracy. When we pulled up it was a huge house on a corner block. One would never think it was a federal halfway house from the outside, but once I walked in, it was completely converted and renovated to house men and women. It was three stories high and a full basement. The men had beds in the basement, which had been made into separate rooms with multiple beds in each room. Also a small cafeteria and an eating area. The first floor was for the director, staff and living room area. The second floor was also housing for men and the top floor was where the women stayed. I was given a bed in the basement and assigned a counselor. Then I was given strict rules that upon breaking, would be a fast ride back into incarceration for my remaining months. We would be given a pass each day to look for employment, plus we were given one hour each day to leave for leisure time. If we were one minute late we could be violated and sent back to prison. With permission, we could have a vehicle, as long as we verified a valid driver's license and insurance. The main objective for the halfway house was to help us transition into society, employment, family and environment.

My first pass was the next day, I was given eight

hours to go to the DMV for license renewal, car insurance for my vehicle that had been parked at my parents in the garage. I went to AT&T and bought my first smartphone. By saving money from my commissary job, painting portraits and family helping, I had saved a couple of thousand dollars to help me establish myself. I also bought hygiene and clothes for myself. I needed to look presentable for interviews.

The next day I was given a pass again. This time I had my parents pick me up to look for work. In the parking lot of the mall in Pleasanton, I tried driving for the first time in years. Within a few minutes, it all came back to me. So many new things to learn. Phones with the internet, Wifi, and Facebook. I also spent time with my two older daughters. Over the next few days, I was able to see my brothers also.

By dinner time, everyone with day passes had to be back in the house. The only reason a resident could be out, was if they had jobs during the swing shift. The eating area was small, so within a few days, I began to meet some of the other men and women in the house.

I sat with a few of the guys, one of them said, "So David, what are you plans once you get out of this place?"

"Well, the first thing I want to do is find a church to attend," I said.

He laughed, surprised by my answer. "Come on, bro. I get it, you found it better doing your time reading a Bible, but seriously. You'll forget about God within a month."

This time I laughed at the comment. It was just a friendly conversation over dinner and I realized that many that come out of prisons do exactly what as he said. It's called leaving the Bible at the release gate.

"You know, I get what you are saying. When I got arrested in 2004, I surrendered my life to Jesus. And many told me that once I was sentenced I would forget about God. Well, I was sentenced in Sac and taken to Santa Rita Solitary. Then many said once I was out of the hole, I would forget about God. I finished my time in solitary and went to Terminal Island and continued to follow Jesus. Then I was told that once I left Prison and made my way to camp that I would forget about God because the politics and prison tension would no longer be there. So I transferred to the Atwater prison camp and stayed serving the Lord. Now I am here, having dinner with you, and you are saying the same thing. God has done way too much for me, I could never forget and walk away from him," I said.

His laugh changed into a serious facial expression.

Then he nodded. "I can respect that, I was just joking with you. I really hope you continue, man."

I replied, "It's all good, no offense taken."

A few weeks passed and I continued to look for work. I now had my car parked at the halfway house which made it easier to look for employment. I was learning to navigate my way on my iPhone, and making calls to some of my friends I hadn't heard from in years. I would text my oldest daughter every single day. I found a website for artists and began a profile along with photos of the paintings that I had brought along. I also began attending a different church each Sunday. I had no idea where my home church would be. Each time, as soon as service was over I would walk straight to the pastor to introduce myself. I would let them know that I had just released from prison and that I was looking for fellowship. Most of the pastors gave me their numbers and I would call or text them regularly. Part of the halfway house program was going to counseling each week, as a group and individually.

One day I was given a five-hour pass to look for work. I decided to drive to the Stoneridge mall in Pleasanton so I could go from store to store putting in applications. I began to have mixed feelings about my passes outside of the halfway house. While on one hand if felt nice to be free, driving down the freeway and doing things normal civilians did, I couldn't shake the awkward feeling that I no longer belonged in this free world.

As I walked through the mall asking for applications or opportunities for work I decided to rest on a bench. As I sat there I noticed families walking together, couples, friends, and groups of people laughing, talking and smiling. I felt so out of place. Suddenly I didn't want to be here anymore. I wanted to be back in Atwater with the brothers. I began to wonder what they were doing. It was lunchtime so I figured they were all in the cafeteria, sitting in our regular tables and laughing in fellowship. All of these years I longed to be free, and now that I was free, the world felt different to me.

I tried to take my mind off of Atwater. I remembered something one of the officers in Atwater told me. He knew who I was as Sir Dyno, and often asked me questions about the music industry. One day he told me that A.L.G., one of the members of our rap group had also become a Christian. I wondered how I could get a hold of him.

I began to feel panicked with so many people in the mall. I began to pray. "Lord, I don't know why I feel this way. I miss Atwater, I miss the brothers. There is nothing out here for me anymore. If it is true that A.L.G. is serving you, Lord, please make a way for me to communicate with him. I don't know where to begin."

Once I passed my three-month mark in the halfway house, I was given an ankle bracelet and allowed to live in Tracy at my parent's house. Things were going smoothly as I continued in my college courses. I spent hours sitting in the living room talking with my parents, brothers, and children. The brothers in Atwater and Terminal Island never left my mind. I wrote them letters so they knew that I was doing okay.

One day I heard a knock at the front door. I had never imagined seeing this person ever again. It was Young Ant, another of the Darkroom Familia artists on my label. Somehow he emailed me and I had answered back. He had heard that I was out of prison and had wanted to see me. His real name is Anthony, and I asked him to come in. He introduced me to his wife, Angel and their two children. I was so excited to share that I was now a believer of Christ, and he shared that he also had surrendered his life to the Lord. We began to fellowship and share the things God had done in our lives. We talked about old times and how far we had come. He was living in Tracy for the time being, so I told him he could come any time to fellowship. I let him know that I was wearing an ankle bracelet and I couldn't leave unless it was for work. We sat for hours and for the first time in months, I felt great in being able to talk with someone, aside from family about the things of God. Finally toward the end of his visit.

"Remember A.L.G.?" asked Anthony.

"Of course. I heard some things in prison from a guard. I don't know if it's true or not," I answered.

Anthony nodded. "What did you hear?"

"I heard that he also surrendered his life to the Lord also. But I have no way to confirm it or get a hold of him."

"Brother, David. I have his number. And to answer your question, yes he did give his life to the Lord."

The minute Anthony and his family left, I called A.L.G.'s number. There was no answer, so I decided to leave a message.

"Hello brother Tony, This is brother David. Please call me back."

Within a few minutes, my phone rang.

"Hello," I said.

"Hello, who's this?" asked Tony.

"It's me, David. I just got out brother."

I began to explain to him everything I had been experienced over the last few years. I shared with him about Anthony giving me his number. I didn't give Tony a chance to respond as I talked and talked about everything God was doing and going to do. Once I was done I heard silence.

Tony said, "David, I'm really happy about everything you are telling me. I can't believe it. But to be honest, I'm not doing so well. I haven't been to church in a while. I'm married now with some kids. I wish I could tell you I was doing better, but honestly, I'm not."

My heart dropped. I was so busy telling him all God was doing in my life that I didn't bother to ask him before I rambled on. I just knew that Tony was going to be a big part of my Christian walk, as well as Anthony. God was about to do something special and I was not going to let go.

I said, "Tony... listen to me, brother. I don't know what you are going through, and it doesn't even matter. All I know is that we are going to serve God together. We have a lot of work to do for the Kingdom. So get your boots on and tighten your laces."

Tony stayed silent on the other line. Then said, "Thank you, David. I appreciate you calling me."

"Can we talk again soon, brother. I want to meet up with you as soon as I can."

Tony didn't hesitate. "Of course. Call me anytime."

I met Tony and his wife Sylvia a few days later,

along with my cousin Carlos. Soon after they both re-dedicated their lives to the Lord and we began to plan ministry soon after.

During the first year, I was invited to speak at various churches because of my status in the underground scene. First Stockton, then Gilroy. Before I knew it, I was sharing in Victory Outreach San Jose with over 1,000 people listening.

There is a saying in prison for guys getting out. It was, 'be careful because you've been locked down so long you'll fall in love with the first smile you get.'

As strong as I thought I was, this also happened to me. A year after my release I was married. After being away for so long, every inmate wants to immediately jump-start their lives all over again. We want to make up for lost time as if it's a race. I had met someone early on of my release, saw the smile, and just as the saying goes, I fell for it.

I include this in my story because even though I was strong Biblically, it doesn't mean I am perfect. We all learn and grow as we continually renew our minds. Our discernment also grows and we get wiser as time goes by. If you are reading this while incarcerated, and you have a release date. Please remember this one thing. Rash decisions in prison can cost you your life. The decisions you make when you get out, apply to the same rules. The problem lies in having no contact with a woman during your entire sentence. You are punished if you look a woman officer in the eyes. You desire a nice conversation or going to dinner, or hearing nice affirmations from a woman. Yet upon release, meeting a woman instantly blurs your decision making. It creates cloudiness where you need clarity. I married a woman that I felt had the same heart for God as I did. I believed I was equally yoked. In my bad discernment, I was convinced she was the one I saw in my dream. On our wedding day, I handed her the sealed letter I wrote in Atwater.

A week after the wedding I launched House of Rest Church in Modesto California. The first service was at a banquet room of a hotel. Within four weeks, I realized I could not afford to rent it each Sunday and opted to open a house church. Being newly married, we needed a bigger home. We figured it would work out for the best. I found a big Victorian home with a basement big enough to hold twenty chairs. I knew that the Lord's hand was in everything I was doing in ministry. Within a few months, the basement wasn't big enough. I found a building that was too big for our small group, but I signed the lease anyway. Once we leased the building, we decided to move to Sacramento. This was the beginning of the end. Arguments began to rise up, differences in opinion. The church was struggling, just as any new church has growing pains. Driving from Sacramento to Modesto for Bible Study and Sunday service became overwhelming. Everything began falling apart. As the marriage progressed into a downward spiral, I tried all I knew to keep it together. I reached out to Christian marriage counselors, but help like that can only work if both want it. I did not know what to do, I knew that God hated divorce according to the Scriptures. I had guarded my testimony from the first day I surrendered my life to Christ, and now here I was going to lose it all. I began to feel as if I was failing God. For months I would show up to preach each Sunday and ignored throughout the week. I was willing to stop pastoring, if that is what it would take. She wanted more than that. She wanted to live a normal life without God. That was a line I was unwilling to compromise. I felt hated and despised in my own home. Finally after many months, I had a vivid dream of God releasing me. I wanted to confirm it in Scriptures, and saw this verse I had read many times before.

1 Corinthians 7:10-15 nkjv

[10] *Now to the married I command, yet not I but the Lord: A wife is not to depart from her husband.* [11] *But even if she does depart, let her remain unmarried or be*

reconciled to her husband. And a husband is not to divorce his wife.

¹² But to the rest I, not the Lord, say: If any brother has a wife who does not believe, and she is willing to live with him, let him not divorce her.

¹³ And a woman who has a husband who does not believe, if he is willing to live with her, let her not divorce him.

¹⁴ For the unbelieving husband is sanctified by the wife, and the unbelieving wife is sanctified by the husband; otherwise your children would be unclean, but now they are holy.

¹⁵ But if the unbeliever departs, let him depart; a brother or a sister is not under bondage in such cases. But God has called us to peace.

When I read this passage, I knew I had a clear conscience in the relationship, yet it is clear in verse fifteen, 'But if the unbeliever departs, let him depart; a brother or a sister in not under bondage in such cases.' By the end of two years of marriage, I was handed divorce papers.

I couldn't pay the rent for the building and lost it, and back home in Tracy I was no longer allowed to see my children as much as I would have liked. What did I do wrong? I found myself living in a small RV at my parent's ranch. I was now divorced and having Sunday service at a martial arts school. I thanked the congregation for sticking by me through one of my hardest trials. Each Sunday I would have to put chairs out and the sound system, then put it all away after service. At night in the RV I would have nightmares of solitary. I would spend hours at a time by myself. I felt like a failure. I asked my brother Angel to help me with pastoring the church. He gladly stepped in to help. I was broken, tired and confused. Surely the Lord's blessings were no longer with me.

17

NOTHING IS IMPOSSIBLE FOR GOD

I admit that I can be a stubborn man. This can be a flaw or a strength. When most run away from God when faced with problems, I run to Him. When most become distant from Him during tribulation, I hold on to Him tighter than ever. I had learned how to live with nothing, yet still praise God. What I thought was a curse was actually a blessing. Prison taught me things about life and myself that I would have never learned. It conditioned me to be a plant in the desert with deep roots. I didn't need rain every day to stay alive, I just needed deep roots to find my nourishment. I also learned to trust in God. If he said I would pastor a church and name it House of

Rest, then nothing was going to stop that. If I was going to have a wife someday that wanted to serve God along with me, then nothing was going to stop it.

Before Christ, I helped produce and act in eight films that went to nationwide distribution across the country in video rental stores. I also produced, engineered or performed on over fifty-five albums. It was now time to use my skills and talent to reach the masses. I recorded a project and released it nationwide as a digital recording titled: Dyno – called to reach the masses. It was released on every known platform across the world. I also got together with my good friend and pastor Scott Jungkeit and began writing a movie script. I was relentless in following my higher calling of preaching the gospel, whether by testimony, preaching, the music or film.

My younger son David was being troublesome for his mother, so he was dropped off to live with me. Slowly the Lord was bringing my children back into my life. I now had my son to focus on, which allowed me to rise above the rut I was in. I was able to build a relationship with my daughter Angelyn. I cast her in the movie 'Always With You,' and was able to bond during the practice and filming as we traveled to locations throughout Modesto, Merced, and San Francisco.

Something needs to be said about faith. Here in our western worldview, we see faith as an ideal. A feeling. Yet in the Bible, it is defined as something much more than an ideal. Faith in the Hebrew definition is an action word. Faith is not something you wait on, faith is something you do, believing that your path will open up. When the Lord impresses something on my heart, I don't wait for things to line up. I simply walk forward in obedience. There is a difference of name it and claim it. I don't claim anything, but when He speaks, I go for it.

During this time I decided to take my health back also. I purchased a bike to ride to the gym and realized I loved cycling. It was a time of putting my life back in order. Once the movie was finished I traveled with my son to different churches to premiere the film. Many times the churches would provide a hotel for us to stay at. At times we would take our bikes and ride the trails in whatever city we were in.

Even though the House of Rest church was still meeting in a martial arts school, it continued to grow. I was able to see the grace of God in my life. He was still with me. With my brother Angel helping me pastor the church, we were growing strong.

Months passed as I stayed focused on my son, my

health and the church. Before I realized, two years had passed since the divorce. Even though I continued to press forward, I often wondered about the dream the Lord had given me while in Atwater. I figured in God's timing, maybe He would bring someone special into my life.

One day, I posted a photo on my Facebook of my coffee drink. It was a 'Cadillac,' which was a prison delicacy. While in Sacramento County Jail, sugar was not allowed. Many of the inmates would make illegal pruno to get drunk, and sugar was one of the main ingredients. On Commissary, coffee was sold and was too bitter to drink black. So to sweeten the coffee, I was taught to make my coffee and drop a snickers candy bar into the cup. The chocolate would melt, the caramel and the coffee would taste as smooth as a Cadillac. I continued to drink coffee like this when I was released.

Someway, through a Facebook mutual friend, a woman named Sharon saw my photo of my Cadillac drink. This brought on curiosity, due to the fact that she baked vintage and eclectic style cheesecakes to sell. She was always on the lookout for new flavors to try. She decided to ask me questions about it, this then turned into daily conversations. I learned that she had been serving God for over two decades and sang on the worship team, and most importantly single. She held a prayer night in her home each week and had been a part of many ministries over the years at the same church. She lived six hours away in the San Fernando Valley in Southern California. I had never met a woman like her. Once she was comfortable with me, she shared a dream she had just three days before she saw my post of my coffee drink. My jaw dropped as she described meeting a man that lived out in the countryside with three brothers. She had no idea I was living at my parents ranch surrounded by tomato fields, and I had three brothers. The more we spoke the more I realized that Sharon was the blurry woman in my dream without a shadow of a doubt. After a few months of continually talking on the phone, she came up north for two days with her son so we could meet in person. I set up a place for her and little Abraham to stay, so she could meet my family, and of course deliver some cheesecakes. Finally, after some months, I drove down to Southern California with my son David to meet her pastors, this was of 2015.

As I write this book, it is now 2020. We courted for three years, and have been married for a little over two years and look forward to many more together. We have recorded more songs together, we have a daily devotional that we do together on

Youtube, we cycle together and are each other's best friends. This is not to say that life is perfect. We have gone through some tough times together over the last few years. I had to nurse her back to health, along with close friends after she had a brain surgery. I was also hospitalized and taken into an emergency surgery which caused a long hospital stay in San Francisco. Many times we face financial obstacles that most would never guess. Not because we put on a mask, but because we trust in the God we serve.

Many times as Sunday service begins, I look up to the stage to see her always standing on the right, leading worship. Only this time, her face is no longer blurry. Recently we just moved into a bigger building that has double doors into the sanctuary. My favorite thing to do during practice is to walk into the double doors, like my dream, just to see her. I am in communication with all of my children now and am a grandfather. I have seen God do amazing things in people's lives and I feel that this is just the beginning. My parents now attend House of Rest and they are able to see the promise God gave them when I was a child.

Anthony (Young Ant) and his wife Angel are currently youth leaders at House of Rest with a calling from God for so much more. Tony (A.L.G.)

and his wife Sylvia also lead a small group and are also leaders at House of Rest church. It still amazes me that three men from Darkroom Familia rap group are now together, serving Jesus under the same roof. We know and believe that more from our past group will come to know Jesus also.

Just remember, If God can change a man like me, He can change anybody. Nothing is impossible for God. I urge you to not only learn about who Jesus is, but just as urgently learn who you are in Christ.

To the inmate reading this, please get your heart right while incarcerated. Become the man or woman that you are meant to be. All of hell will hit you like a tornado when you step out of prison. If you can't walk now, how do you expect to run with the horses?

To the young person reading this. Please don't take my story as something to glorify. I know many that lost their lives while incarcerated. Prison is not a place I would wish upon anyone. It takes one single mistake to lose years and decades of your life. And while you are in a cell, your friends and family will be in the free world living on with their lives. Your boyfriend or girlfriend will go on living and be with someone else, while you sit in your lonely cell. The best thing you can do is to pursue God with all of your heart. He will guide your steps when you put your trust in Him.

One time I was spotted at a gas station by a Sir Dyno fan. He walked up to me with a curious look and asked,

"Aren't you Sir Dyno? Man, I'm a big fan of your music. I have every CD you ever released!"

I had never thought about how I would answer this question until this moment. I made me think the same question to myself. Am I still Sir Dyno? Before I realized my answer, my words were already coming out of my mouth.

"No, Sir Dyno died. He drowned in the baptismal tub in federal prison... But my name is David. That was who I was in the past. If you got time I'd like to share how it happened."

And this became the way I would answer this question every single time I was approached. Which still happens today no matter where I go. The prophetic Word I received from my Tia Benny was spot on. She said that the Lord was going to show His power through me and that I would reach many for Jesus. No matter what the enemy has planned for our lives, God is always steps ahead. I am convinced that Jesus enjoys making a fool out of satan, by getting the broken, destroyed and rejected and making these rejected into the strongest warriors this world has ever seen.

To the believer, I pray that this book blessed you

and encourages you. Maybe you know someone that needs to read it. Please don't hesitate to pass it on. Maybe the Lord will use this book to tug at someone's heart in a way that you've been unable to.

To the fans of Sir Dyno. I appreciate you so much. You have followed my music, many of you from the beginning. If you have lost a loved one because of violence, I am truly sorry for your loss. I do ask this of you. If I had just an ounce of influence with you, then please let me urge you to seek out Jesus Christ. Only He can take the pain, the struggle and the weight of life. Many have said that I left the homies. No, I didn't. I am using this book to come back and say there is a better way. There is no reason to live in darkness. The Bible says that Jesus came to shed light in the darkness, and the darkness couldn't comprehend it. Open your heart and be honest with God. Those that seek Him will find Him.

To my family, children and my wife. I love you all so much. I couldn't have done this without any of you. You are my support and my pillars. Thank you, dad, for surrendering your life to Jesus when I was young. This gave me something to aspire to. Mom, thank you for standing on the promises of God for me, my brother Angel, Steve, and Ruben.

Sharon, I know that I am not an easy man sometimes. We have both been through pain and suffering before we met each other, and together. Yet, God always makes a way for us. I know that the letter I wrote and sealed didn't end up in your hands, and for that I am sorry. But without a shadow of a doubt, I know you are the one I prayed for when I walked the track in Atwater. But I offer something better than a letter, I offer you myself and the rest of my life.

God bless you all, in Jesus' name.

Contact information

David & Sharon Rocha
www.houseofrestchurch.com
email: houseofrestchurch@gmail.com
Youtube channel: David Rocha

OTHER AVAILABLE TITLES FROM PARAKLETOS PUBLISHING

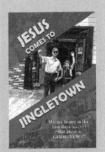

Midst of My Confusion
by David Rocha

God's Fingerprints
by Alfonso Gomez

Jesus comes to Jingletown
by Dale Trujillo

Called out of Darkness
Music Single
Featuring Dyno, Young Ant
A.L.G., Syl, Sharon, Rose

God is Faithful
Music Single
Dyno featuring Sharon

Always With You
Feature Film
Available on YouTube

For more information go to:
www.houseofrestchurch.com

252

Made in the USA
Monee, IL
24 February 2022

91784143R00142